Acknowledgement

I would like to thank my mother, "Sharon Smith," which is the love of my life. I have learned so much from watching her life, in fact her life inspired me to write this book. She came from an impoverished background, and she has always had the spirit of a rich person.

To my son, Kendall Wainwright – you are my motivation.

To my other son, Jonathan Wainwright Jr. – you are the adrenaline that keeps me going.

Finally, to my only daughter, Alexus – you are the courage I needed to keep going and not quit. This combination of inspiration, motivation, adrenaline, and courage has contributed to making a supernatural being.

INTRODUCTION

YOU WERE BORN RICH

The fact remains that it is not possible to live a complete and successful life, unless one is rich. No human being can rise to their greatest possible height in talent or soul development, unless they have plenty of money.

The purpose of existence is growth! There is nothing right about living in poverty. The world is an inexhaustible storehouse of riches, of which the supply will never run out. This book is designed to teach you how to become rich, and how to regain your mental wealth that was lost through the domestication of American teaching.

The American educational system teaches you to work for paychecks, pay taxes, save money, and invest in long term stocks, and you will be... comfortable! That's brain washing slavery! It is that educational system, that has stolen your prosperity, wealth, and your thought process through training you to think only on the level that provide ways for the rich to get richer.

This book teaches you how to use your own thought process to make yourself rich, where your economic wealth provides you with the freedom to choose the lifestyle you want to pursue. This book also focuses on self-achievements. Such as: starting your own business, showing you how to be your own boss, how to establish yourself in this new information age, and how to replace your current salary with income generated from your ideas.

Building your own business requires patients, dedication, and perseverance. However, the rewards are well worth the time you invested. Your initial goal should be to create enough revenue sources that you no longer have to depend on a paycheck, or selling your time for undervalued wages, while someone else is getting rich off of you.

The only thing that separates you from people who are financially successful is: they have already found the knowledge contained in this book, and you have not done so... yet!

You can tell when a person is very wise, by the questions they ask. You can also tell when a person is very clever, by the way they answer questions.

Jonathan Wainwright

JACKPOT PUBLISHING PRESENTS...

Cracking The Millionaire Code

"THE SECRETS OF HOW THE RICH GOT RICH"

#1 Financial Guide in the World

By:

Jonathan Wainwright

Copyright © 2019 Jonathan Wainwright

All right reserved. No part of this book may be reproduced in any form, or by any means without prior consent of the author and publisher, except brief quotes used in reviews.

ISBN: 9798588137522

Book Production: Crystell Publications
You're The Publisher, We Help You
Self Publish Your Book
E-Mail – minkassitant@yahoo.com
Website: www.crystellpublications.com
(405) 414-3991

Printed in the USA

DEDICATION

This book is dedicated to everyone that has been a part of the struggle. Especially those who always wanted better out of life but didn't know what roads to take in search of financial freedom. Now comes "Cracking The Millionaire Code" which is the road to your financial success!

Jonathan Wainwright

Jonathan Wainwright

CRACKING THE MILLIONAIRE CODE

PART I

SELF KNOWLEDGE

Jonathan Wainwright

THE POWER OF IDEAS

You have the ability to develop ideas without blinking, ideas are what rule the world, learning to use the mind, Ideas will come to you in seconds, and will give you the tools and the know-how to bring your ideas into fruition that translate into '$uccess.' Ideas are inventions, ideas are products, factories, wealth, health, everything that you see in the world today came from an idea, and you have full access to any ideas. One of the reasons people are stuck in poverty is their lack of courage to express their ideas, remember ideas come from the mind, they do not come from you or anybody around you, and all ideas are valuable, and if used in the correct fashion, they will make you very rich.

> "What you think about, is what you bring about."
>
> Never postpone your dreams, or delay putting your ideas into action! You must implement your plans (blueprints) immediately!
>
> "If I can only remember everything I forgot, I would already be rich!" - JACKPOT!!
>
> "All that we are, is the result of our thinking!"
>
> "If you can see it in the mind, you can hold it in your hands."

The mind never forgets anything, just when you thought you forgot something the mind pulls it out of its storage and hands it to you. The mind can remember things that happen in your life as a very young child, things that you may have forgotten. The mind still has a clear picture of it, as if it just happened seconds or hours ago. This may come as a surprise to you, but the mind does not belong to you... The mind belongs to GOD.

> "Everything that you see with your eyes comes from somebody's ideas, why not use your own ideas to create massive wealth for yourself."
>
> "Ideas become riches when you express your courage to make them happen, most people are in doubt of their own successful, ideas."
>
> "All the wonders of the world was once ideas, now they are phenomenal masterpieces, whose creation cannot be explained, even with today technologies."
>
> "When you learn to use the mind to draw out ideas, you become the most intelligent person you know."
>
> "The only way to accomplish anything is with bright ideas, which are yours, waiting to be recognized by you."
>
> "The mind holds all the ideas that ever existed: past, present, and future, waiting on you to translate them into success."

THE MIND IS NOT YOU

"GOD's mind is the only reality."

The mind and the brain are two different things. The brain is an organ inside of the body; While the mind is not inside the body. The mind has created everything in the world, including the brain and the body.

The good book says GOD created you in his mind first. There is only one mind in the world, and that is GOD's mind, but we are all partakers of this one mind. Meaning GOD allows us to use that same mind to accomplish whatever we wish, whether it is riches or poverty, happiness or misery, health or sickness, GOD's mind is a bank of wealth, a storehouse of knowledge, information, health, business plans, blueprints, riches, prosperity, thoughts, energy, and ideals. Just waiting on you to make a withdrawal of whatever you wish.

Most of us have the misconception that the mind belongs to us. Have you ever heard someone say: "You have been on my mind" or "My mind told me not to go over there." The mind is not yours; the mind is not you.

"Every human has the same access and connection to GOD's mind."

"There is not one problem on earth, you can't solve once you have become problem conscious of your true self."

GOD's mind is everywhere at the same time, in everybody, and in everything, including you! We are all one, so when you aim to hurt someone else, you are actually aiming at yourself. Once you realize this, then envy, jealousy, and hatred exit your life.

"You have to learn how to use the mind correctly and withdraw the things that your heart desires."

What is it that you wish to withdraw from the mind? Is it wealth? Health? Riches? Money making ideas? Knowledge? Information? Whatever it may be, the mind has it in abundances, just waiting on you to realize that you were born rich. You were born with perfect health; you were born with access to all the knowledge and information in the world.

Remember, it is the mind that has all of this in abundance, and it created you!

> "The mind is the supplier of everything. The mind is like a bank, waiting on you to make withdrawals of whatever you like, whatever you love, or whatever you desire. Right Now!"

Have you ever heard of a situation when a frail old woman pick up a car to save her child that was trapped under it. Or, the story of two young boys ages 10 and 11 that was outside playing, when one of them got trapped under a very big log. That is when the other boy was able to pick up the log with one hand to grab his brother from under it. An adult man witnessed the, whole thing in amazement, and came back the next day with 5 other grown men and together, they tried to move the big log, but could not even budge it! The mind was at work in both situations.

> "The mind is the single most powerful thing on earth, but you must learn to take advantage of that advantage."

> "All successful people have learned how to use the mind in ways to make themselves, super rich." You can too!!

> "People do not just wake up billionaires, they have learned to use the mind to achieve great success."

> "The day you were born, you had an advantage on life, and have been unconsciously using the mind throughout your whole life, now it is time to consciously use the mind to gain health, wealth, and anything your heart desires."

> "Being aware of the mind and learning how to use it, is

life transforming."

"The wealthy have always known these facts and have went to great measures to keep this knowledge away from you."

"Any person can become rich if they will just learn how to use the mind, the mind rules everything around you, if you would just learn to use the mind constructively." The Sky is the Limit!

HOW DO WE USE THE MIND

You must first educate yourself on how the mind works, the mind flashes over 60,000 images to you everyday. The mind operates under the 'cause and effect system' the mind cannot reason inductively, meaning it does not know the difference between right, wrong, good or bad. The mind is like the magic genie, it is giving you exactly what you want through your thinking process. In other words, whatever you think about the mind is giving it to you, whether it is good, bad, right or wrong. So, you must learn to control your thoughts. Many people unconsciously think of poverty and sickness, but do not understand how it showed up at their front door. Their thoughts were the cause, because the mind produced it, so the poverty and sickness were the effect of those thoughts.

> "Suffering is always the effect of wrong thinking - good thoughts can never produce bad results, just as bad thoughts can never produce good results."

> "Thoughts can become the jailer of fate, thoughts can also imprison you, or they can easily become the angel of freedom, thoughts liberate!"

Cause and effect is how the mind works. Your thoughts are the cause of everything life hands you, and whatever life hands you is the direct effect of your thoughts. That is the reason you must guard your thoughts and only allow prosperous thoughts to enter the mind. The mind will produce whatever you allow into it, good, bad, right or wrong. So it is up to you as to what your life comes out to be. You hold the key to your life.

> "You have to learn how to think the thoughts of things happening the way you want them to happen."
>
> "Remember, controlling your thoughts is controlling your world, again people do not just wake up in prison, or wake up in the crazy house or wake up billionaires -- NO! -- Using the mind correctly or incorrectly puts you there."
>
> "Nothing just happens by chance everything is cause and effect, the mind is the cause, and what you see, or experience is the effect."
>
> "Money making thoughts are what must be developed and sent to the mind so you may withdraw success and prosperity."
>
> "Every thought of yours is a real thing, thoughts are energy."
>
> "You have drawn everything to yourself, your whole life has been a manifestation of your thoughts, which is energy."

The mind is supposed to be used to advance the human race, the mind can do any and all things, the mind can build you mansions, uncountable amounts of wealth, health, love, friendships, happiness, enjoyment, the mind can have you stress free, worry free, doubt free, and financially free. First, you have to gain the knowledge of how the mind works and learn how to apply that knowledge to your everyday life. The mind is all powerful, unchanneled power waiting to be channeled by you in the right direction for your success!!

Airplanes have always been inside the mind, wireless telephones have always been inside the mind, boats, trains, spaceships, cars, computers, the internet were all built inside the mind, before they came into physical form. Electricity was not invented, it had always been in the mind, but somebody learned how to use the mind to make it work in the advancement of the human race, and you can do the same thing by using the mind to advance your own life.

> "The outcome of you is whatever you choose." -Learn to set the course of life, do not just blow in the wind, take control and head to the roads of success.
>
> "Do you want to succeed, or just get by? The door to wealth is not easily opened, you must force your way in."

You must be conscious of your thoughts; you must know what you are thinking at all times and have control over your thoughts. You must only think of the things you want and learn to block out the thoughts of the things you do not want. Because thoughts are energy, the old saying "thought are things," the world is an energy field, the sun which we believe gives us light, is pure energy, it is giving off energy not light, just as the sun's energy penetrate upon things, those things grow in hopes of reaching their full potential. The mind energy also penetrates upon things, those things are thoughts. Remember thoughts are energy, so when the mind is thinking thoughts; that energy goes out into the world, which is an energy field, and those thoughts must come back to you (in real life), which is your outer lite, the thoughts and energy is your inner life. (Mind).

Whatever is being made or thought of in your inner life (mind) will appear in your outer life (real life), you can create bad situations, just as fast as you can create good situations for yourself, and most of the time it is done unconsciously, you do

not even know that you are the one bringing these situations into your own life.

> "Each thought is energy; each active thought is active energy; concentrated thought is concentrated energy; thought concentrated on a definite purpose, becomes power."

> "The person that learns how to control their thoughts, and learns to direct the energy, gets anything out of life they wish. This person has learned to command prosperity and has become the master of the mind. Therefore, life now caters to them; money is now chasing them; prosperity is in their every step."

> "The mind has the answer to any question in the world and can solve any problem in the world."

Doctors have agreed that medications and treatments do not heal the body, only the mind does. The biggest help to doctors is to help the patient trick the mind into believing that the medication is working, so the mind will reverse what it has done and start the healing process. Doctors have been known to make pills out of sugar or salt; give them to patients suffering from cancer or other deadly illnesses. Then, two or three days later, come to the patient and play his/her role in helping trick the mind by saying the pills are working well. Once those thoughts reach the mind, the mind begins the process of healing the body, because that is how the mind works, it produces whatever thoughts are planted into it, good or bad. Now you know how important it is to control your thoughts, which is done through practice and concentration.

> "What are you attracting into your life right now? - Just look around you, that is your answer."
>
> "It takes the same amount of energy to create one dollar as it does to create one million dollars."

VISION

"Whatever you are visualizing, and you have that clear picture in the mind of exactly what you want, you are using the mind to bring those exact things into your life."
"Rich people visualized themselves rich before riches came to them; Whatever you visualize will materialize."

We lose our vision to be greater in life if we do not take steps to make them come true, you must learn to concentrate all your thought energy on making your vision come true. "Thoughts, implies service," meaning if your vision is to open a car dealership, the mind immediately starts to work out ways to make your vision happen, the best part of this is the mind starts to do it unconsciously, -without you- but you must work with the mind in order for your vision to manifest itself in real life (your life) working with the mind implies taking control of your thoughts and directing your energy in the direction of your vision, and holding your thoughts and your vision at the front of the mind for long periods of time without letting other thoughts barge in and interrupt your vision. Again, thoughts imply service or action. the mind will command these actions into real life processes, starting with everything it is going to take to start your car dealership. First thing would be research, the mind will lead you to researching every aspect of owning a car dealership. Next would be how to obtain the licenses necessary to operate a car dealership. Lastly, you will be able to find out how much capital will be needed to start the business. That is why it is important to hold your vision at the front of the mind for long periods of time, because the mind will be working on every aspect that is needed to bring your business into fruition. Remember, the mind is the cause of everything, and your car dealership will be the effects of the mind through conscious controlled concentrated thoughts, which in itself is power. The mind is also going to lead the way in showing you how to obtain the capital necessary to start such a business, learning to use the mind correctly is like having a magic-wand in your hands.

> "Vision is the power to see ideas and use the mind to manifest your vision into reality."
> "Vision is our ability to see into the future, when you start visualizing wealth and health, they start moving closer to you."
>
> "When you use your vision to mentally see things happening those things start to appear in your life's journey." Visualizing is the seedling of reality!
>
> "Visualizing is very important, it is one of the first steps to achievement, it is also the visual pictures of your thoughts."
>
> "Everyone visualize whether they know it or not, visualizing is the key to success." "Nothing can stop our vision from coming to you... But you!"

Many people think visualizing is playing with your imagination, but in reality, it is a preview of life's coming attractions. Whatever the mind can conceive, it can achieve.

Wealth is all about your thought process, is all about how you think. Success comes from within, not from without. The mind is the creator of all that exists. When people are completely focused on what is going wrong, subconsciously they are attracting to themselves more situations that will go wrong.

OUR EDUCATIONAL SYSTEM

> "The type of education that is in traditional schools is 'not' what the rich use to get rich."
>
> "The American Educational System is not teaching entrepreneurial education, they are teaching our kids how to work for other people or big companies, and how to climb the corporate ladder, but they are not teaching them how to own their own business."

Most of the greatest entrepreneurs who ever lived, did not attend college, or they dropped out of college. For example: Thomas Edison, founder of General Electric; Steve Jobs, the man behind Apple Technologies, which is now a trillion-dollar company; Mark Zuckerburg, the owner of Facebook, the largest social media network in the world; Henry Ford, the inventor of automobiles, and the founder of America's largest automobile company The Ford Motor Company; Walt Disney, the founder of Disney World in Florida, and Disney Land in California, which is the largest tourist attractions in the world. All of these great people did not attend or dropped out of college and went straight into business, entrepreneurship, inventions, and investing, all of these tycoons created trillion-dollar businesses and profited billions.

"I am not telling you not to attend college, but I am telling you college is not needed to become a great inventor, entrepreneur, or investor; which are the richest people in the world."

"Sadly, in America, which is known to be the richest country in the world, over 80% of the United States Population is at the bottom of the financial ladder."

"You will never know true freedom until you achieve financial freedom."

The educational system must change by teaching people about thought energy. Life has always been about thought energy, from the time of the prophets, to the time of kings and queens to the present time of governments, they all have used thought energy. Technology was created through mental energy projection, and the use of thought has been a very tight kept secret by world leaders and world rulers. The people in this world that "do not" use thought energy are stuck in poverty, sickness, fear and worry, our educational system does not teach you how to think wealthy, instead they train you how to think the same way you would train your dog to do tricks. Our educational system is not teaching you about you, and how to direct your energy for your own personal gain.

"School is a 'SYSTEM' that teaches you how to make money for other people, not yourself, schools do not teach real life financial situations, a public education will teach you almost nothing about money."

"School gives you the skills to perform certain jobs, but it does not teach you how to be successful."

"Most people spend their life working for other people

> or companies with nothing to show for all their hard work, you have just made somebody else rich." That's SLAVERY!!
>
> "Never take advice from someone who is not where you want to be in life."

If someone is not practicing what they are preaching, then do not follow them. In other words, if someone is not already doing what you are trying to do, you should not take advice from them, teachers are employees, they cannot teach you how to be an entrepreneur, many people dropped out of business school, because of that fact. They are not practicing what they are preaching, in reality teachers are teaching you how to be a great employee, a CEO of someone else's company and how to climb the corporate ladder to being a number one employee.

> "An employee cannot teach you how to be an entrepreneur, you must focus your time and energy on what matters the most - Financial Freedom!"

ROBOTS TAKING OVER

The rise of the robots is coming! As technology moves into the future robots and artificial intelligence is taking the jobs of millions of people, people that are thinking about career jobs are delusional! Robots have already started taking the jobs of fast food workers, medical doctors, accountants, journalists, teachers, bank tellers, and many more areas of the work force. Mass unemployment has arrived, you must become an entrepreneur, or investor and let those robots work for you, they do not need sleep, food, vacations, sick time, or days off; they work 24/7 for zero pay and benefits.

"Why go to school and major in a profession that robots and artificial intelligence are taking over." That is not financial education.

"Be smart in this new age of thinking and ideas and capitalize on new advancing technologies, the world is changing you have to be first in line to change with it."

"Elon Musk owns Telsa. One of the most innovative automobiles on Planet Earth. His cars only use electricity, not gas. The factories that manufacture these automobiles have over 300 robots in each factory. That is more robots than human beings in these factories. Once upon a time those jobs were occupied by human beings. In the next 10 years, there will be no human beings working in these factories, they will all be replaced by robots. The takeover is reality. We must start investigating what our schools are teaching, because they are not teaching real financial education. Soon robots will be the teachers in schools, and governments will be paying very low wages for adults to stay home, because there will be no jobs to go to. Robots will have taken all of them over."

"When you walk inside any store, and you see self-checkout registers. Those are robots that have taken a job that use to belong to a human being."

"Robots are not chunks of metal built to look like humans with arms and legs.. No! They are artificial intelligence which is technology that was built to replace human beings in the workplace. Such as: Toll Booths: where you use to drive up to a human toll booth worker and give them the toll fees. Now almost every toll booth is automated, with no human being in sight."

THIS BOOK

Many books tell you how to get rich, but your riches will not come anytime soon, those books are telling you a 40/50 year plan on how to get rich. You will be nearly at your death bed when the money starts to roll in. "Cracking the Millionaire Code" is about making the money right now! While you are young enough to enjoy it.

> "Money is about power! Money can turn your dream into reality."
>
> "You either use money, or money will use you; you must master money, or money will master you; money is a game of reality."

THE TRUTH WILL SET YOU FREE

I know you have heard that saying many times, but never had any idea what is the truth, or what it will set you free from. Well the truth is you have the same blood type, DNA, Spirit, and mind as GOD. Yes, the mind that you use is GOD's mind, you just do not know how to use it. GOD created you in his image, and his likeness, that means he created you identical to himself. Your mind is GOD's mind. Where do you think all your ideas and thoughts come from? They don't come from you, they don't come from other people, or animals. They come directly from GOD's mind, so let's think about this for a second: If all your thoughts come from GOD's mind, and you are able to use the mind, then that means there is nothing in this world you cannot do. There is nothing in this world I do not know, there is nothing in this world you cannot be! That is the truth that sets you free, now you are free from worry and uncertainty, from fear of not being able to be successful - Life is an unfoldment!

"This is not a religious book, but a book of truth, GOD created you in his imagination, which is the mind."

"You were created in the image of GOD, and in his likeness. The definition of image is: A reproduction of the form of someone or something; an optically formed duplicate; a close or exact resemblance to another or double. The definition of likeness is resembling, being alike in appearance."

"Okay, let's look deeper into this: If you can use GOD's mind to do anything "why are you broke?" Maybe you are using the mind to stay broke. What are you using the mind to do? You can have anything! One of the first things we must do is get away from our domesticated thought process that tells us poverty is a part of life, learning the truth about yourself is the most important thing you could ever do!"

"What will the truth set you free from? Worry? Fear? Stress? Or self-doubt? Most of us go through life worrying about survival, paying bills, putting food on the table, running in fear of how to survive financially, stressing about never being able to get ahead, which all leads to doubting yourself and your ability to achieve success. But, knowing the truth about yourself will eliminate worry, fear, stress, and self-doubt."

"Your lack of knowledge of self is what has kept you in bondage. When you learn about your true identity, you become free of all of life's baggage, such as worry, fear, poverty, sickness, regret and many more. It is then you will start to understand you were born rich, but you have been intentionally domesticated, which means there have been systems put in place to keep you from knowing your real self. America's educational system is at the top of the list.

"You have to break free from those domesticated teaching and get back to the original being that GOD created, which is identical to himself."

"America educational system made you believe you were just a victim of circumstances, situations, and conditions, when in reality; you are the maker of them."

"If you wish to become wealthy in this lifetime, you must first learn the truth about 'you'."

Which is: You are not the flesh!

UNFOLDMENT

"We can have whatever it is we choose; I don't care how big it is. Knowing that it already exists in the mind, all you have to do is unfold it."

Unfoldment means to bring something out that is already there, everything in life that you need or want is already inside the mind, but you alone must bring it out. You were born rich!!

You were born with all the knowledge in the world, such as, science, mathematics, chemistry, geography, and all the information contained in the books in the world's libraries, because you had access to the mind, even at birth. Life is an unfoldment, which means you have to bring this knowledge out, a good example is: Electricity. Electricity has always existed in the mind, but we had to bring out the understanding of it, and how to use it for the advancement of life. The mind can do the same thing for you. The mind will give you the blueprints to good health, wealth, happiness, and the focus to be whatever your heart desires.

"The mind has the key to every situation, but the question is 'what will you do with it?' Most people have only unfolded poverty and self-destruction, which comes from domesticated teachings. You must learn to unfold prosperity, health and wealth."

"Life is an unfoldment, meaning everything you want already exist, you have to learn how to unfold them from the mind, extremely wealthy people have always known this secret and used it to make themselves very rich."

"If you ever learn how to unfold your visions and ideas, the world will view you as a supernatural being because success and prosperity will be in your every step."

"GOD's mind is invisible, but you can see it in everybody, everything and everywhere, the mind can make you invincible!"

"Only one percent of you can be seen, the rest of you is invisible and untouchable."

FOCUS

"To be financially successful, you must focus on your mission and pursue it until completion."

"Focus is being able to see what other people can't see."

"A locksmith will not do you any good because the

real wealth is locked inside you. And you alone hold the keys." Focused Thinking.

Focus has been known to stand for "Follow One Course Until Successful." We must learn to focus at all cost. If we are to become a success story focus is absolutely necessary, without focus, you will become a failure, focus means to put all your attention on one subject. Driving a car without focus, you will not reach your desired destination. It is the same in life, you will not reach your goals of success and prosperity without focus. The lack of focus will leave you standing still while the world is passing you by.

> "Focus is being committed to a single purpose, one aim - focus unifies energy and power and make something strong that was once weak."

> "Anytime you focus on something action starts to happen, as if you had a magnifying glass and focus it on anything it would start a fire, when you focus on anything the mind starts to make it happen."

> "Focus takes practice with all the outside distractions going on in the world, it's hard to focus on one thing at a time, if you have visions of success, you must learn to focus."

> "Once you learn the truth that sets you free, focus will come easy, worry, fear, poverty, and sickness will no longer be a distraction and your ideas will unfold masterfully."

REAL LIFE

"Being broke and being poor are two different things. Being broke means that you are temporarily without money. Being poor means that you have no idea you were born rich or how the mind really works."

"Never allow what you cannot do, stop you from doing what you can do."

Your life is like a big slab of marble, and you hold in your hands the chisel and the mallet. Will you hammer out a masterpiece? Or will you destroy the slab of marble into millions of useless pieces. You can make whatever you wish out of your life, the world is waiting on you to chisel out success. But, whatever your knowledge is of how the mind works, is exactly what the world will see from you. You can become like the doctor that created "Frankenstein" who eventually destroyed the doctor that created him, many times in life we do just that, we create - manufacture - or indulge in things that will eventually destroy us. However, we can chisel out great wealth and success like Jeff Bezo did with Amazon, he hammered out trillions of dollars from an idea that he withdrew from the mind, you yourself can do even greater things if you will only learn to use the mind correctly.

"We have been given dominion over this world, but most people are letting everything in this world have dominion over them."

"If you will only wake up to your real self, poverty will not exist. As long as you are asleep at the wheel, you will always be a victim of your surroundings. Life events will happen to you, not for you. You will become a floormat to the world, in order to be rich, you must think the same way the rich think, and that is knowing your true self."

"Life is a harsh reality, because you cannot blame anybody for your life events, but you. We all have lost control of our life at least one time since birth. Most have regained control through focus, vision, and recognition of self. Knowing your life is in your hands and you can make it into whatever you wish, is the truth that sets you free."

THE MIND AT WORK

"While the body is asleep the mind is still working, dreaming, thinking and controlling the heart, it is also controlling the blood pressure and everything inside and outside the body." **So, how powerful is the mind?!**

The mind runs everything in the body, if someone told you something that made you mad which is a mental state, the mind will control the body by making the blood pressure go up and making the heartbeat faster. If you receive information that makes you mad, sad, or glad the mind will control the body to do different things. When hearing sad news, the mind tells the body to slump the shoulders and shed tears. When the body gets hot, the mind makes the body sweat, which is an attempt to cool the body down. The mind will have you experiencing euphoria and ecstasy in happy situations. The heart is a muscle that must be controlled by something. Your blood pressure must also be controlled by something. Well, the mind controls all of it, even when you are asleep the mind is still working, if not, your heart would stop beating, and your blood pressure would go out of control. So the mind never sleeps.

When a person gets mad about one thing, the mind opens a

flood gate with all the things you could be mad about. You start thinking about things in the past that have made you mad. It's like the boss at work who gets mad at one employee about taking a very long cigarette break. Next, he is coming after you about being late, then he goes after another employee about her dress code. It is the same way with being happy, the flood gates open, the mind is just running, pushing thoughts out everywhere, so many images are flashing, thoughts are running wild, it's hard to control this type of mind, but you must learn how to do it if you want prosperity. Prosperity does not come by accident it must be achieved.

> "Learning to control your thoughts is a process that requires much practice. Try to think of one subject for 3 or 4 minutes without letting another thought enter the mind... After you try it, you will see that practice is very much needed."

> "You have to get rid of all the bad, hateful, evil, envious, jealous thoughts and develop good prosperous money-making thoughts."

> "The world thinks the sun is giving off light, but in reality, its giving off pure energy, when the mind is at work, it is giving off one thousand times the amount of energy as the sun. Remember, the mind created the sun."

> "The mind is the tools of life, what will you build with life tools. Will it be success or destruction? It is totally up to you!"

> "The mind is controlled by your thoughts, so what are you thinking? Riches or poverty? Sickness or health? Life or death? Success or failure? Whatever your thinking, the mind is giving it to you."

OPPORTUNITY IS YOURS

"It does not matter where you come from. All that matters is where you are going - Land of opportunity."

"People are anxious to improve their circumstances but are unwilling to improve themselves."

Nobody is poor because opportunity has been taken away from them, opportunity is all around us! Most people cannot see those opportunities, because they use the mind on the useless things of the world, or they believe the world is monopolized by other people. However, it is the opposite that is true, opportunity is on every corner of the world, most people don't use the mind in the right fashion to seize the opportunity, there are so many different businesses and blueprints inside the mind, if you would only apply yourself. Opportunity is not just given to you, but you must create opportunity. You might ask: "How do you create opportunity?" Through financial education, you must educate yourself about money. Traditional education will teach you nothing about real life money issues. Once you are educated in that area, then you cannot be denied, because you just created an opportunity for yourself. The only thing that can stop you, is **you!**

"In order to earn more, you must first learn more. Learn to turn opportunity into wealth."

"Most people believe opportunity has been taken away from them, because they don't understand that GOD wants you rich. So opportunity will never be taken away. Just as rich soil will never stop producing what is planted into it, the mind works the same way, you must plant opportunity into it, and opportunity will be yours on every corner of the earth."

"The way you see life is exactly what you get from it. If you see disaster, your life will be disastrous, and disaster will become your shadow, and follow you everywhere you go. But, if you see opportunity, it will be your day and night. No exceptions."

"With such great wealth in this world, nobody should ever remain in poverty. You have to learn to. take advantage of every opportunity"

GOD WANT YOU RICH

"GOD did not create the human race so that we may be poor living in poverty. The planet is full of riches. Everywhere you look financial riches are there. People are getting rich from other people's trash through recycling. So think about it: if trash can bring you riches, then any and everything can bring riches to you. 'Creative Thinking' is where wealth begins in the application of thought."

"Prosperity only comes when you are ready to receive it, the world is waiting on you to understand GOD wants you rich, you were not created to be in poverty."

You must get rid of the thought or idea that GOD wants you to be poor, or his purpose might be served by keeping you in poverty. NO! GOD wants to increase your life by giving you everything the world has to offer, that is within the realm of positive love, happiness, and integrity. This means GOD wants you to be RICH!!

The desire for riches is simply the capacity for larger life seeking fulfilment. This is GOD's plan. That which makes you want more money, is the same thing that makes the plants grow, which is life seeking fuller expression. It is the desire of GOD that you should be rich, not suffering in poverty. That is why he gave you the understanding of how to use the mind. So you can think thoughts of prosperity, and then have them manifested into your life! You have to learn the truth and stay away from those old, domesticated thoughts that tell you GOD wants to punish you, or take you through hard times for things that you have done. None of that is true! GOD actually sheds tears when you do not know how to use the mind to achieve life's great wealth that is on every corner of the earth. You actually take yourself through hard times and punish yourself because of your lack of knowledge of one's self.

> "GOD gave you knowledge, wisdom, and understanding, but your true understanding of these three have been flawed by a misunderstanding that GOD wants you to struggle in poverty. When in reality, GOD gave you knowledge to uncover your true identity and wisdom to know you are one and the same, and for you to have understanding that through the mind you are communicating with GOD, and he is giving you your heart's desires."

CAUSE AND EFFECT

"Whatever thoughts you send out into the world will

bring those exact circumstances right back to you. So if you want money, love, power, or happiness, those are the thoughts you have to send out into the world."

"For everything that happens in life there is a cause of why it happened, and what you see happening is the effect of that cause. The mind is the cause of the thoughts you send out into the world which then causes the effect, which is your life's situations."

"Most people only look at the effect or the situation that is happening not realizing there is a cause as to why the situation is happening."

"Most people believe themselves to be victims of the circumstances surrounding them. Not knowing they have created those very circumstances through cause and effect."

You must become the master of the mind and learn to control your thoughts. The mind has been compared to a garden and a jungle - a jungle is actually an unkept garden - the gardener must tend to his garden all day, everyday, so weeds cannot sprout up and overtake the harvest by turning the garden into a jungle, where weeds choke the life out of the fruits and vegetables, killing the harvest. You must be the gardener of the mind and keep all the weeds out or keep the bad and useless thoughts out of the mind. Whatever is planted, will grow and produce whatever was planted, so you cannot plant poison ivy and expect to get strawberries. You cannot plant cactuses and expect to get oranges. It is the same with the mind. You cannot plant envy and expect to get riches. You cannot plant jealousy and expect to get love. You cannot plant hate and expect to get happiness. Whatever you want out of life is exactly what you must plant into the mind. Whatever you plant is the cause of life's situations and circumstances. Thought is the action of the mind, when it is used correctly, you become the master of self, which is the ruler of the world.

> "Learning to control your thoughts is learning how to think of one subject for long periods of time without letting other thoughts barge in."
>
> "You might be saying 'I didn't think this bad situation into my life.' And you might be right, but you might have wished it into someone else's life, or entertained it unconsciously, remember your thoughts are like a boomerang, you push them out only for them to come right back to you."
>
> "You have to realize you are the cause and effect of your own life, you become the author of your own conditions (good or bad). The mind is the greatest gift GOD extended to us to use to enable us to reach the highest level of life in every way: wealth, love, happiness and everything this world has to offer."
>
> "Every situation or circumstance is the effect of a cause. Cause and effect are the workings of the world. Your thoughts are the cause of everything in our life's path, the effect is all the situations and circumstances you encounter in your life's path."
>
> "The mind makes everything happen. You learning to use the mind, is you controlling your future."
>
> "Living under self-limiting beliefs leads - to failure, which leads to not believing in cause and effect, once you understand cause and effect, your whole life will change and so will your situations and circumstances."
>
> "The inside world is the cause and the outside world is

the effect. The inside world is the mind and your thoughts; The outside world is where you see the effects of the mind (your real life). What is going on in the inside world is also going on in the outside world. The outside world is a reflection of the inside world. If the inside world is in chaos, then the outside world is very chaotic. Meaning, if the mind is receiving successful thoughts, then in your real life, you are a very successful person, because your inside world (cause) is screaming success, so your outside world (effect) must follow success!! If your inside world is screaming hate, evil, deception and lies, then you outside world is full of pain, heartache and misfortune. These are the laws of attraction and the laws of success."

DESIRE

"GOD would not have given us a yearning desire for achievement without giving us the ability to achieve them."

"The heart's desire is the reason for all wealth attainment. Desire puts energy and motivation into thoughts."

"Desire is something that is naturally inside of you. It is the starting point of all achievement and the first step towards riches."

Desire is something that all human beings have, something that GOD gave to all of us. Desire is nothing more than wanting things, which is normal for all of us. GOD created things and gave us a desire to want them. GOD wants every human being to experience every perfect thing that he created. Desire is also a big part of the law of attraction. When you desire something, you begin to attract it to you. Desire is a natural part of your genetic makeup! To desire is to obtain, to aspire is to achieve.

> "If you want something very bad, it is called a burning desire. Desire immediately set the course for you to obtain your goals and dreams.
>
> "GOD gave you a desire for every good thing in the world. He also gave you a way to own every desire you might have."
>
> "Every human being who reaches the level of understanding the purpose of money wishes for it. But wishing will not bring you riches. Having a burning desire for, riches becomes an obsession, and learning to use the mind with a burning desire, the mind starts to create definite ways and means to acquire riches, and those ways and means will never recognize failure."
>
> "A wish is not a burning desire; a burning desire is the ability to want something more than you want everything else. Every person that desires to win must be willing to cut all sources of retreat, meaning there is no turning back!"
>
> "Desire is the first step towards wealth and the first law of gain. All achievements, no matter how big or its purpose, must begin with an intense burning desire for something definite. Whatever it is you can have it."

THE POWER OF YOUR WORDS

"You can literally speak things into existence. So be

careful what you say, because it will show up in your life."

"Never speak bad words to people or about people, because those same situations you spoke about will end up falling on your head."

"When you speak words of prosperity and success, they immediately show up in your life path."

The power of words also has energy forces behind them. GOD spoke things into existence and since you were created in his image and in his likeness, your words carry weight. So be careful how you use them and where you direct them. In most cases words are like boomerangs, you throw them out, only for them to come right back to you. So do not wish or throw bad words at other people, keep all negative words out of your mouth, because those negative things will end up on the same road you are traveling in this life.

"Use the power of your words to achieve great prosperity and success, not destruction!"

"The invisible forces of the power of words is always working. GOD spoke the world into existence, if you wish someone bad luck, you will surely attract bad luck to yourself. If you wish to aid someone to success, you will be aiding yourself to success."

"Usually, people are speaking what they are thinking. You should only use your words for three purposes: to heal; to bless; and to prosper. Speaking good words towards life will produce a great aura of protection. 'No weapon formed against you shall prosper.' Never speak ill words about someone unless you want those same forces to rain on you. Words have vibrating power; they begin to attract."

KNOWLEDGE IS MONEY

"You must become rich in knowledge, before you can become rich in real life, uncountable wealth is the manifestation of using knowledge correctly."

"Financial freedom is obtained through the use of knowledge, your financial and prosperity level will never rise above your level of knowledge."

"You have to know exactly what you want. Then plot the course of action (blueprint), get started, and you will arrive. However, if you never get started, you will never arrive at the land of prosperity. You will always have destruction, confusion and poverty at your doorstep. When you wake up, that blueprint must be in your thought process, and you must be chipping away at it every single second. Knowledge is the key."

"You must become a wealth builder and start creating blueprints that are road maps to riches."

Knowledge is information that is used for advancements and success. Once knowledge is acquired, the world changes, and once the world changes, money changes hands.

Knowledge is power, politicians express their power everyday from the knowledge they have acquired over a period of time, you can do the same thing. Gathered education equals knowledge, we are not talking about traditional education, we are talking about financial education.

Learning = Knowledge = Wealth
Gathered Education = Knowledge
Applied Knowledge = Wisdom

WISDOM CREATES WEALTH!

You must be able to make sense of the world when others cannot understand it. There is a power under your control that is greater than all your fears and worries combined. It is the power to use the mind correctly and direct it to whatever you wish to see accomplished, applied knowledge is the answer.

The knowledge of business equals money to the person that has gathered this business knowledge. You can gather any information on any businesses and then educate yourself to that business. Which becomes a working knowledge of that business, and that alone equals success, riches and great wealth.

> "Prosperity is based on new information, new ideas and knowledge, before you can become wealthy you must think like a rich person and obtain the knowledge that rich people use."
>
> "Wealth is the offspring of knowledge that has been organized into definite plans of action and directed towards a definite end."
>
> "Knowledge becomes power, only when it is applied. GOD did not create you to be in poverty. Creative thinking and the application of knowledge equals riches beyond your wildest dreams."
>
> "The person that knows 'how' will always have a job. The person that knows 'why' will always be their boss.

Information is the most valuable asset for any investor."

THE REAL YOU

In order for the world to see the real you, certain things must happen. You must get rid of low self-esteem, lack of confidence, self-doubt, fear, worry, hatred, jealousy, misery, lack of ambition, limited thinking, and anything that could tarnish your shine. Then, and only then, will you be able to recognize your true potential, and realize you are GOD's greatest creation.

CRACKING THE MILLIONAIRE CODE

II

THE GREAT NATURAL LAWS

GREAT NATURAL LAWS

"The Law of Opulence: Means having wealth, having much, or plenty, and this law belongs to you by birth. You inherited this law the day you were born. It is yours to have for free, all you have to do is recognize your true self."

"The Law of Attraction: Means having the ability to broadcast energy and become a magnet and draw to yourself anything your heart desires. Again, the recognition of this law puts a magic wand in your hands."

"The Law of Abundance: Means you were born rich, and you are entitled to abundance of everything you wish to put your hands on. GOD wants you to have everything the world has to offer. That is why he created it all just for you!"

"The Law of Supply: Means that anything you desire, there is a supply at hand waiting on you to direct thinking energy intelligently, and draw your desires to you, again through your birth you inherited these laws, they belong to you."

The law of supply says you should never want for anything because the world has more than enough for every person. The world is waiting on you to recognize it belongs to you. The government of the United States is printing trillions of dollars annually. Why are you broke and struggling financially? The simple answer is you do not know anything about the law of supply.

The law of abundance says you were born rich. But you hold poverty thoughts of yourself, so these riches are running away from you. Mentally, you are stuck in a life of struggle and poverty. How can you want to be rich, but always think poor thoughts? What you think about becomes your reality. The law of attraction says you have the ability to draw wealth, health, happiness, love and joy to yourself. Instead, all day long you think about envy, jealousy, hatred, worry and fear; consequently, that is what keeps popping up in your life's path. Why not attract to you what you want, instead of what you do not want.

> "Learning to use these great natural laws will turn you into the person you always thought you should be."
>
> "The very wealthy has always known these laws and live by each and everyone of them daily. When a person is poor in their thoughts, they are also poor in their pockets."

THE LAW OF ATTRACTION

The law of attraction is the ability to think thoughts and have those thoughts become real life. The mind is like a receptive station, it is transmitting and receiving energy frequencies, but it is only receiving your thoughts and transmitting back to you exactly what you are sending out. So if you are sending out love, you will get love back. If you are sending out success and prosperity, then that is exactly what you will receive back. The law of attraction is an operation that will magnetize the things that you are thinking about to end up in the palm of your hands. Vision boards are great tools to exercise the law of attraction, humans are always drawing things to themselves, or pushing things away, mostly it is done unconsciously. It is just as easy to push success and prosperity away from you, as it is to attract it to you.

> "All laws work together for the advancement of the human race. Success can be yours through the law of attraction. Right now, at this very moment WHAT ARE YOU ATTRACTING TO YOURSELF?!"
>
> "You become a magnet, and you start to magnetize wealth, success, and prosperity, the law of attraction becomes like a genie that is saying 'Your wish is my command.'"
>
> "If you are sending out hatred and evil, then you are magnetizing pain and hardship into your real life. You have to control the thoughts you allow to enter the mind."
>
> "You become a transmitting station; your thoughts send out energy forces that is drawing back to you whatever you are thinking about. Thoughts create vibrations of mental forces, consequently it is the most powerful tool in existence."
>
> "The law of attraction is working even if you are not conscious of it, your thoughts are magnets."
>
> "The leaders of the past, such as kings and queens have always known about the law of attraction, but choose to keep the masses ignorant by domesticating them through educational systems."

THE LAW OF OPULENCE

The law of opulence is absolutely unlimited! The word

opulence means: great wealth, extravagant, and lavish. Opulence belongs to you by birth! You can only limit opulence in your own life through your perception of life, meaning the way you see life when it comes to money, wealth, or riches. Some people see themselves as being rich in the future and riches will come to them in the future. Some people see themselves as being rich right now, and as a result, they have millions of dollars right now. Most people see themselves as being broke, or being a struggling employee, or living in poverty. You are exactly what your perception of life is, but you can change all of that by learning the law of opulence. Which is: Health and wealth is due to you, in the present state of the world, knowledge and the recognition of opulence is on the unconscious plan. The world does not know about opulence, and the ones that do, are not telling.

> "The law of opulence says all you have to do is wake up and realize your true self, which is the making of a GODLY King. Through birth you inherited riches, wealth, abundance, and life which is all the world has to offer."
>
> "Why are you still living in poverty, when the world belongs to you? Why should a very rich man starve to death when he has great wealth at hand. (This is you!)"
>
> "What else needs to be said to you, or done to you for you to understand your true self? How many more degrading situations have to come upon you before you realize the truth about you? You have "not" because you know "not" of what is at hand. You become like a blind person that know everything around them exists but cannot see it. You are blind to your true value, and the source of your creation."

"These great natural laws are the teaching of your true being, everyone needs to learn all they can about oneself."

"Know thyself," is one of the greatest commandments, the more a person truly knows and understands themselves, the more you know the truth about the great laws. Then you realize you are one with these great laws and the laws exist for your advancement.

"Learning the law of opulence puts great wealth in your hands, stress and worry fades away, and financial freedom invade your whole being."

THE LAW OF SUPPLY

No one is kept in poverty by a shortage in the supply of riches. There is more than enough riches for the whole world. The United States alone has enough building material to build every family on earth a mansion twice the size of the White House. The world has an inexhaustible storehouse of wealth, the supply will never run short, if individuals are poor, it is because they are not using the mind correctly and do not know anything about the law of supply.

"There is nothing right in poverty, you must think of abundance, opulence, plenty, positions of power, growth and harmony."

"Knowing your true self is knowing that every desire or want you experience, there are more than enough supply that you may have it 10 times over. You are never kept without because of a shortage in supply."

"Poverty is one of the worst diseases in the world, it

will cause you to suffer every day of your life, until you realize the law of supply is the cure.

"The essence of this law is you must think abundance, opulence, and success, visualizing what you want, your desire for it will recognize the supply is waiting for you. Remember, the future is of your own making."

"Operating in absence of these great natural laws is like begging for failure, knowledge does not apply itself. You must make the application."

TRUE FACTS

Humans have depreciated themselves through the lack of not knowing their source of life, and how life actually came about, once you learn these fact, you instantly realize nothing can stop you from becoming the greatest the world has ever seen, self-crushing has been the method of every previous system of training, starting with our educational system, intelligent understanding of these great laws, and how to cooperate with them will bring you the most beautiful successful life you could imagine.

When you set the mind to a task in the right order, you must, and will be successful through the law of attraction. Just as the law of gravity exists, the law of abundance, the law of supply and the law of love, also exists. You cannot believe in one and not believe in the others. You are like a magnet; you attract to yourself what you think about the most. Think your tomorrow into existence today, thinking of how you want tomorrow to turn out, you are creating your life intentionally. Many people feel stuck or confined by their current circumstance, and feel like it is their only reality, this comes from not knowing the power of right thinking. Humans master their own destiny by first changing their thought process. Every time you say "I'm broke, I do not have any money" or "I cannot do that," you are creating yourself to be all of those things.

> "It has long been said you were created in the image and likeness of GOD, and have GOD's Power and potential to create your world, and you are doing it every second of the day."
>
> "When you look in the mirror, what you see is the tip of the iceberg. If you looked at your body under the proper microscope, you would see that you are not solid, but a bunch of microscopic pieces held together by energy."
>
> "Everything in the world is made up of the exact same thing, the human body, trees, the oceans, the moon, the stars, the whole universe, our galaxy, the planets, and everything in the world is vibrating energy, nothing is solid."

You are energy. Energy is described as something that can never be created or destroyed, it always was and always will be, everything that exists now has always existed. Everything is energy moving in and out of form, you are a spiritual being having a human experience, "NOT" a human being having a spiritual experience. Let me explain it this way: You are the most powerful transmission station in the world, you can broadcast energy, meaning you can send out or take in energy. You can transmit energy waves and bring to you anything in the world because everything is energy. Nothing else in the world can do that but you. (Spiritual being)

"Understanding how to direct energy, you can cause anything you want to vibrate to you. Energy can never be created or destroyed, but it does change forms."

"If you took the DNA of the tree outside and took your own DNA, it would be a match, because everything in the world is made of up of the same thing: 'Energy'."

"Nothing in the world is solid, everything is small particles held together by energy, the mind direct energy in the form of thinking and you alone control it."

"Spiritual beings manage their own magnetizing energy, nobody else can do it for you. Millionaires have been using energy to bring themselves riches."

"Knowing your true self is knowing you were born rich, and knowing inside the mind you already have your heart's desire. You just have to see yourself with it, the world is waiting on you to recognize your true self, which is a spiritual being."

"Governments of today have set up information blocks and try to keep you from gaining this information of these great natural laws."

CREATING BLUEPRINTS

"You must change your way of thinking and commit yourself to million-dollar plans (blueprints). The poor struggle for survival, the middle-class fight for comfort and security, the rich enjoy financial freedom because they utilize blueprints with the help of the great natural laws."

"The mind has billions of blueprints waiting for you to

withdraw them so you can become wealthy and financially free."

"Most people only want to devote 10% of their time and energy in the pursuit of obtaining their dreams, this is a recipe for failure. Set your thought process on successful blueprints, using the mind, while putting the great natural laws in action you become invincible."

"You have to set clear goals and a timetable for their completion, utilizing blueprints will allow you to be able to see success where other people see failure."

After your blueprint, there must be a plan of action! Nothing from nothing, leaves nothing! You must become a doer, and not just a talker. You must be a person of action, not just a planner. You must become an entrepreneur and not a wannapreneur. You must mentally be able to see your next move, or it will not happen. Mental imaging is everything, conventional thinking is old industrial age thinking. You must realize in order to be successful; you have to be a new information age thinker.

"When you create a purpose (blueprint), power comes out of nowhere and inspire you to accomplish. Masterfully, you become an army of one. You must set goals with clear plans (blueprints) of executing them. Setting goals without blueprints and a course of action is setting yourself up for failure."

"Most people want to know: is there a blueprint one can follow to get rich, or become successful and have prosperity? The answer is: 'Yes.' But the mind already has the blueprint, the problem with you and success is 'You.' The mind is waiting on you.

Formal education is not needed in the pursuit of riches, but you must be willing to listen and learn, and you must understand that the accumulation of riches cannot be left up to luck, chance, or good fortune. However, the accumulation of riches is obtained by knowledge, innovation, study, concentration, new ideas, financial education, and the application of the mind. Remember the mind is a bank of wealth, knowledge, ideas, riches and prosperity, all you have to do is learn how to make withdrawals from the mind. It has whatever is needed for your journey to prosperity.

> "When applying new age information, you must learn financial education, reading books is a must. Become a student of wealth, formal education is not necessary to become rich, but you must learn entrepreneurship and have a desire for knowledge and new information. You have to learn the language of money, and study how other people got rich and use their knowledge to further yourself." Wealth Equals Freedom.

> "You will either live your dreams, or drown in your failures. Proper preparation (blueprints) is the key to financial success. You must create a new and improved 'You.' Wealth is not the result of some guarded secret but the use of the great natural laws and clarity of purpose." Wealth Demands You To Grab It!

> "Organized knowledge is the formation of blueprints, and blueprints are required for the accumulation of money. Organized and intelligently directed knowledge is power! Power is necessary for the retention of money once it has been accumulated."

> "Organized thinking is mentally building blueprints for success. You must become free economically and

financially, or you will never be free personally. 10% of the people in the world make 90% of the money in the world. Most people are not financially educated."

"Millionaireship begins with never wasting money on items that depreciate the very second you pay for them. I do not believe in living below your means, but I do not believe in foolish spending either."

POWER AT WORK

The Power of Concentration: to make a success of anything you must be able to concentrate your entire thought upon the idea you are working out. You must learn how to hold one thought or idea in the mind for long periods of time without letting other thoughts interrupt you. Do not be discouraged if you cannot do it at first, you must practice and continue learning how to concentrate on one subject at a time. This brings focus to that subject, which then manifests your thoughts and ideas into your real life without delay!

> "Success is definite when you learn how to concentrate. You are then able to utilize constructive thoughts and shut out all destructive thoughts. Learn to think only of what is beneficial."
>
> "We accomplish more by concentration. All real advancements will come from your concentrated efforts."

The Power of Love: thoughts covered in Love is Power! With this power, you can manifest anything in your life of your choosing, by being of good character and positive thought. The best way to create riches is to create systems that make money for other people, and in the process creating wealth for yourself.

> "Love is the strongest force in the world. It can accomplish anything on the planet. Thoughts that are motivated by love are unstoppable. Love has created everything in existence, it is faster than the speed of light or sound, it has more pressure than all of the

water in the oceans."

"Sending out love, you will surely get the same back in return. Remember, life is like a boomerang, whatever you send out in mental energy, you will receive it back in your life path. So learn to think thoughts covered in love, because through the law of attraction, you are attracting to yourself, all the things you think about."

"Love keeps negative thoughts out of your thought process. Most people have negative thoughts everyday, mostly about other people. However, you cannot achieve great level of success with this train of thought. Regardless of what that person has previously done towards you, you must not let that person rob you of your mental assets. You must become a humanitarian and love the world and everybody in it, this is the only way to overcome negative thoughts, which ultimately leads to negative actions, which also leads to self-destruction."

GOD's first and last name is love. GOD also says, "you must love everyone in the world, equally, or more than you love yourself." Now that is true power! Once you come into the understanding of this knowledge, you can do anything in the world. You can walk on water, you can fly, you will become the full image of how GOD imagined you in his mind. GOD created the birds, so we know he can fly. He parted the sea, so we know he can walk on water. He also created you in his likeness, this is the truth that sets you free. Love is the key to success, and the key to life.

The Power of Success: Success is absolute! The key to success is learning the thought process faculties. In what degree do we use them? Some people use them to get rich, while other use them to chase poverty. Everything that has ever been accomplished in this world was accomplished through the power of success. The power of success is using the great natural laws covered in the power of love and the power of concentration.

> "You can overcome poverty with the power of success! Most people think themselves into poverty, you can use the power of success to eliminate poverty."

> "You can be anything you want to be through the power of success. 'Self-Made' wealth has always belonged to you, if you would only set your thought frequency on success the power is in you."

> "Make every thought a successful thought. Make every action a successful action. Form a clear concept of what you seek to accomplish, after using your thought faculties, and a blueprint of action, success becomes definite."

> "The road to wealth is having a burning desire for success! Learning to concentrate puts focus on success. Focusing on success manifests great wealth in the hands of great thinkers."

FEAR AND WORRY

> "Fear is something that people have been dealing with forever. Fear plays tricks on you, only because you do not know it does not exist."

> "Worry is another thing humans have been dealing with since B.C. Worry is something that you are dealing with in your own thoughts, because what you are worrying about probably will never come true."

"A person can worry to death about things that will never happen. Most of us worry about things that might happen, and not about things that has already happened."

"The person who conquers fear and puts away all worrisome thoughts, will become "Free." Life does not start until one is absolutely stress free."

"Remember your thoughts are energy forces that goes out from you to the situation that you are thinking of (The law of attraction) whatever thoughts you plant into the mind will produce the seeds you planted, even if it's bad, good, worry or fear."

"You reap what you sow - in other words: you get whatever you plant, if you plant worry you will get destructive situations to worry about. If you plant fear you will get situations that will turn your hair gray overnight, or situations that will run your blood pressure up in seconds. If you plant prosperity, you will receive riches. If you plant health, you will become the healthiest person in the world. The truth is: fear and worry only become real when 'You' make them real!"

"If you want situations to change, stop worrying, and start thinking different thoughts of that same situation, then the outcome will change. You can change the outcome to whatever you want it to be by changing your thoughts."

"The law of attraction allows you to change a negative into a positive. You are the maker and creator of your situations, circumstances, and environment. It is all done according to the thoughts that you are planting into the mind."

"Once you learn the great natural laws, and the power of success, concentration and love; then worry and fear instantly die. They were only there because you lack the knowledge of your true self."

"Everyone in life experiences fear. That nagging voice that is always saying 'you will never succeed.' Fear is something that must be conquered on the road to wealth. Fear is only emotions of self-doubt. Fear creates images that do not exist in real life. When fear attempts to grip you, all you have to do is remember the truth; fear is 'False Evidence Appearing Real' not reality!"

"Worry is created by you through your thoughts, and the mind is responding to your thoughts. So whatever you are worrying about will come to you in the exact form of your thoughts. You are the thinker of thoughts, you can control what you think about. You must be the guard of what thoughts you allow to enter in the mind, because the mind will produce whatever enters it."

"Fear will rob you of your health and your wealth. This is another reason for having control of your thoughts. The law of opulence and the law of abundance teaches you that you were born with plenty. Plenty of health and plenty of wealth."

LEARNING FROM FAILURE

"Never be scared to fail, because failure is a learning experience. Failure is actually success in knowing the way you tried it, does not work. Nothing beats trying and taking a chance. Chances make champions. You will never know if you can succeed if you do not try. The fear of failure will stop you from being the greatest of all times!"

"Rich people face failure everyday. Learn how to turn

failure into inspiration; opposition into motivation; rejection into determination. Failure always creates additional power in gaining success. Failures are learned lessons that put you closer to success."

"Failure is the down-payment to success, and is nicknamed 'Wisdom.' Good advice is: 'shoot for the moon, if you fail you will still be amongst the stars.' In order to do something you have never done before, you must become someone you have never been before 'Financially Educated,' failure is your greatest learning experience."

"Failure is a part of success, a very important part. Failure brings out the ingenuity and new ways to achieve success. Do you know of any successful person that reached the top without failure? Rich people have failed thousands of times more than a poor person, but they know how to keep going. You do not drown by falling in water, people drown by staying down underwater.

Failure is the greatest teacher of all times, in fact, failure will teach you more about life and success then spending 8 years in the best university."

THE UNIVERSAL MIND

I told you the mind belongs to GOD. Many people call it the universal mind, but whatever you call it does not matter, what matters is that you know it exists, and know how to use it.

In this book we will refer to it as GOD's Mind, which has created everything in existence, including 'You.' Learning to use GOD's Mind for the advancements of your life is what makes GOD happy. Let me help you understand what all this means. It means that every idea that you have or ever had already existed, fully complete in GOD's Mind. You must learn how to draw those ideas fully complete out of GOD's Mind. Again, GOD's Mind is a bank of knowledge, ideas, inventions, wealth, prosperity, health, happiness, love, and anything you can think of, all waiting on you to make withdrawals from it. Most people call it the 'Supreme Mind' and they are exactly right. The Supreme Mind has an unlimited supply of everything your heart desires, just waiting for you to tap into it and make your ideas become your reality. GOD's Mind will deliver your hearts desires to you through people, circumstances and events. Remember, you are drawing everything in your life to you through directing energy intelligently through GOD's Mind. (Law of Attraction)

> "Now because you are intelligent energy and can direct energy intelligently, you can electrically magnetize anything you want, and bring it to the palm of your hands, once you understand all of this, you become enlightened to the truth that will set you free."
>
> "All power comes from GOD'S Mind, therefore, it is totally under your control, you are the most powerful being that ever existed."
>
> "The flesh temporarily houses a spiritual being (You). You are eternal life, you are GOD manifested in human form. GOD said he created you in his image and his likeness. GOD also said you existed before the world existed. GOD said he blew life into the flesh, which is himself, which is you. You are not the flesh, you are GOD"S spirit, which is GOD himself in a fleshly body. You are eternal life expressing itself as 'You'(In the Flesh). You are the creator and creating the creation of you right now."

Again, you are energy, and energy cannot be created or destroyed. Energy just changes forms. You are pure energy that has always been and always will be. You can never not be, most people think they are human beings having a spiritual journey, but in reality, you are a spiritual being having a human experience.

Q: Who created the Universe?

A: GOD.

Q: Can you describe GOD?

A: Always was, and always will be, never can be created or destroyed, all that ever was, and all that will ever be, always moving in and out of form. Remember, you were created in the image and likeness of GOD, GOD did not create anything else in his image or his likeness, not even the angels.

Q: So what does all this mean?

A: It means that you are so much more than you think you are. GOD gave you intelligence, GOD also gave you dominion over the earth. GOD did not give you poverty or sickness, GOD does not smile when you are broke and sick, those are not his intentions for you. GOD wants you to be rich, and have everything the world has to offer, that is why he created everything just for "You," he gave you all the tools you need to become rich. He gave you the great natural laws, but ultimately, it is up to you to use them. That is why he gave you intelligence.

Q: So what can I use my intelligence to do?

A: Have anything your heart desires.

> "Humans can look into the past and remember things from their past that happen 20 or 30 years ago. Once

you realize you are GOD in a fleshly body, you will also understand you can look 20 or 30 years into the future. You are already creating your future unconsciously, why not learn how to do it on purpose."

"The first question to ask yourself is: 'Who am I?' The answer is: 'GOD in a fleshly body.' The truth is: 'So is everybody else.' GOD'S life is in every person in the world, the flesh is not you, so you are really just GOD's life. Self-discovery, self-mastery, and knowledge of self are key tools to becoming wealthy."

RULES 2 RICHES

"Financial independence is a choice that you have to make. Great wealth must be demanded, expected, assumed, and thought of, before you can see it manifested."

"Learning is a lifelong experience, you must learn to turn stumbling blocks into stepping stones, and turn dreams into reality."

"Avoiding risk is equal to avoiding opportunity. Risk is the price you pay for opportunity. You cannot avoid risk and hope to enjoy financial freedom. Risk is an essential part of progress.

"Controlled risk is the offspring of creative thinking, wealth is thoughts, creative thinking is the gateway to financial success."

"Never borrow money to buy the appearance of wealth. There is a big difference between being rich, and just looking rich. Most poor people love to have the appearance of wealth but financially they are losing.

"There have been many lives wrecked on the road to

wealth, but financial education is your insurance policy against financial ruin."

"If you plan to be rich, you must expand your knowledge of wealth and rethink your belief system. Never focus on what you are going through, focus only on what you are going to do."

"When you change your mind toward things and people, things and people will change towards you. The person that sets their thought process on acquiring wealth must be prepared to make great personal sacrifices."

"You must see yourself doing it. Everything that has been built or invented, existed in the mind first, but someone seen themselves doing it, making it, in possession of it, using it, and then created it! So anything you want out of life you must see yourself with it, in whatever shape you desire having it. Understanding the power of concentration can help you see yourself with it. Always remember whatever happens within, manifests itself outward; so whatever you think about inside the mind, eventually shows up in your real life. Thought is energy, and that energy projects forward."

"The main things that make us wealthy in this lifetime is 'Free.' The most precious resource we all have is Time, use it wisely, and to your advantage."

"Happiness, health, and prosperity are the results of right thinking. Wealth is in ideas, but you have to seek it by thinking correctly. Visualize what you want, your desire for abundance, opulence, and success, will recognize the supply is waiting on you. Remember, the future is of your own making."

Most people have only heard of the law of gravity,

but these other laws are just as sure and proven as the law of gravity. Poverty is not the answer, just like charity is not the answer. If you give a hungry man a fish, he would eat for one day, but if you taught him how to fish, he will eat for a lifetime. People must be taught about these other great natural laws, and poverty will never exist, but as long as people are uneducated to these laws, they will always look for charity. One has to develop a wealthy thought process, and you can do this by learning how the great natural law belongs to you. They are your birth rights!

"Do not get caught up in the **'Don't Want'** epidemic. Never think about the things you do not want, because you will get them. You must have the knowledge that it takes to build you into a success!" (Ignorance costs more than education)

"Architects draw blueprints, but before the blueprint the architect has to have a plan. We must have a plan, a plan is nothing more than knowledge, a vision, ideas, information, and focus, applied to a business idea. We must learn to put plans together and create successful blueprints."

"Rich people set their own lifestyle and do whatever they want with the world. Poor people are forced into a lifestyle and the world does whatever it wants with them. You end up robbing yourself of a bright future."

"You cannot sit around and expect the government to take care of you. The United States Government is over $100 Trillion dollars in debt, and Social Security and Medicare is underwater and on the verge of drowning. Soon the government will not be able to fulfill its obligations to more than 80 million people that paid into social, security. You must become an entrepreneur in the pursuit of wealth."

"You must learn how to use the mind to be successful. Learn to turn opportunity into wealth. Knowledge becomes wealth, only when it is applied."

"One of the biggest mistakes we make is looking outside ourselves for what can only be found within. We must learn to believe in self."

"Seminars allow you to gain knowledge from experts that have practiced for many years in the field that you are seeking information, which could become a head start for you. Just make sure the experts are practicing what they are preaching, and have been successful in that field."

"The best investment a person can make is in themselves, such as: learning-and gaining knowledge of how to do profitable things and self-improvement."

"There is only one thing that makes it impossible for you to achieve great wealth, and that is: **Fear of Yourself.**"

"If you do not believe in yourself, then nobody else will either. Most people in the world believe in other people's talents and abilities, but do not believe in themselves."(The very second you cease to bloom, is the very second you start dying.)

"You must learn to invest, the rich do it everyday. Investing is different from owning or running a business. Investing is having the knowledge to make money off other people's ideas, systems and skills. Owning a business is working your own ideas and skills. Running a business usually means using someone else system, such as franchises."

"Diversify or die' meaning, never invest all your

money in one asset class, there are four basic asset classes: Business, real estate, paper assets and commodities. You must learn to invest in each asset class."

"Desire is the beginning of all achievements, opportunity is the chance to improve yourself, in your world of thought you can build weapons of self-destruction, or you can build tools that will create prosperity. Vision boards are great tools that will help in building wealth."

CRACKING THE MILLIONAIRE CODE

PART III

CRACKING THE CODE 101

VISION BOARDS

You must learn to create vision boards on you journey to wealth. Everyday you must be able to see, to visualize the very wealth you are chasing, you must consistently view images of what you are striving to obtain.

I used to cut pages out of magazines and newspapers of all the things I wanted to have in my life. I was obsessed with reading articles and publications of the rich and very wealthy, and of their lifestyles, because one day I knew that would be me. You must have your heart set on what you want to achieve out of the life you were given. I used to have pictures of mansions, expensive cars, vacation spots, yachts, jewelry, and many other things of wealth. With vision boards, I can feel this very wealth in my own hands. If you have faith, then GOD certainly has the power!

CRACKING THE CODE 101

MILLIONAIRES FOLLOW THE DATA,
COMPILED INFORMATION EQUALS KNOWLEDGE,
AND KNOWLEDGE IS THE NEW MONEY.

WORLD WIDE WEB

In 1989, the World Wide Web was born. A new age was born, (the information age) the world changed, the industrial age was over, new age thinking came into effect. New ways to make money was born, new ideas that changed the face of the planet. People that continue to use industrial age thinking have went out of business. You must learn how to operate in the global marketplace. With the World Wide Web, Americans are becoming rich selling all their products and services online to every country in the world, knowing how to use the internet to your advantage, which is called **"e-commerce,"** which is a multi-billion-dollar tool in itself will bring you massive wealth. Most people's entire business is on the internet, buying and selling products from one country to another, online stores, online services, online books, web design, stock markets, car sales, real estate transactions, and everything else you can think of is being bought and sold via online. This is where more millionaires are made over night, than in any other business in the world. Most people are working from their personal bedrooms, this is the new information age way of thinking. (e-commerce) At the click of a button millions are made, you do not have to be a fast typist, or a computer genius, all you need is to be willing to make it happen.

CRACKING THE CODE 101

THE WORLD WIDE WEB IS GLOBAL RICHES, THIS IS A TOOL THE RICH USE EVERYDAY TO GAIN MASSIVE WEALTH.

"Are you working hard for someone else, or are you working hard for yourself? Wealth is not something ready-made, it comes from your actions."

"Learning to use the internet for financial gain is new

age thinking. This is financial education."

"White labeling is setting up online stores and selling other corporation's products in your online store for a profit." (Earning a cut of all sales)

"People that were born into the information age do not take advantage of the World Wide Web, they only use it for entertainment and social media, when in reality it is a business tool and a gateway to riches."

HOW MUCH DO YOU KNOW ABOUT MONEY?

Did you know there are only 3 types of income? Ordinary income, portfolio income, and passive income.

ORDINARY INCOME: pays the highest taxes in all three incomes. Employees work for ordinary income, weather you work for yourself, or you work for someone else, it is still ordinary income, because you are working for it.

PORTFOLIO INCOME: is taxed at a lower rate than ordinary income, because it is considered to be capital gain, usually earned in stock markets or flipping real estate property. The art of buying low and selling for a higher price is capital gain, which is known as portfolio income.

PASSIVE INCOME: is cash flow, and taxed at the lowest rate of all three types of income, in most cases as low a zero. Passive income is cash flowing from assets, such as rental property, business, investments, and many other types of assets. Passive investor do not work for money, money works for them.

CRACKING THE CODE 101

WHICHEVER WAY YOU EARN INCOME, YOU SHOULD LEARN TO BUY CASH PRODUCING ASSETS TO MAKE YOUR HARD-EARNED MONEY WORK FOR YOU

ORDINARY INCOME: is mostly earned from a job or some form of labor.

PORTFOLIO INCOME: is mostly made from paper assets such as, stock, bonds, mutual funds, and hedge funds.

PASSIVE INCOME: is cash flowing from real estate, royalties, patents, trademarks, copyrights, licenses, and agreements.

> "Most smart people will turn ordinary income into portfolio income and passive income, meaning people will take their paychecks from their jobs and invest in stocks, bonds, real estate, businesses, inventions, and many other asset classes. Portfolio income and passive income are considered assets, because they put money in your pocket well after you recoup your initial investment, this is known as a level one investor. Wealthy people do not work for money, and one reason is taxes. People that work for money pay the most in taxes."
>
> "If you build a business that can run without you; if you are the owner, and you collect all the profits; this is 100% passive income."
>
> "Self-employed is ordinary income, because you are working for money. The only difference is: you are working for yourself, but you are still working. Self-employed is subject to paying the highest taxes."

"Assets bring money in, liabilities send money out. You must learn to speak the money language in order to have the money conscious."

MAKING YOUR MONEY WORK FOR YOU

The fastest, smartest and safest way to get rich is making your money work for you. So ask yourself: "How do I make my money work for me?" The quick answer is: Become an entrepreneur or investor. Entrepreneurs are generalist that build businesses and hire specialist, such as managers, CEOs, CFOs, and build a team and teach them how to work together for one common end... "PROFITS"."

An investor is someone that invest in the business that the entrepreneur has built, in most cases, investors provide the start-up money for the business. As the entrepreneur is building the business, the investor gets paid through profits and shares of the company's stock, and then they turn around and make billions by selling those shares through the stock market and IPOs. The investors also receive tax breaks and tax incentives; while the employees of that same company, receives crumbs in the form of paychecks; only for the IRS to hunt them down and demand large percentages of their paychecks. The entrepreneur and investor walk away with the lion share of the profits, paying almost "zero" in taxes, they receive multiple tax write-offs for every expense they encounter. Learn how to do what the rich do, use the government for your own personal gain, and enjoy depreciation by making your money work for you.

CRACKING THE CODE 101

JOIN THE RANKS OF MILLIONAIRE, BILLIONAIRE, TRILLIONAIRE CLUB BY MAKING YOUR MONEY WORK FOR YOU, NEVER WORK FOR MONEY, LEARN TO BUILD BUSINESSES, OR INVEST FOR PROFITS

"Making your money work for you is real financial education. Learning entrepreneurial skills and how to invest is the smartest thing you could ever do."

"Your biggest investment should be in yourself. Surround yourself with like minded people who share your passions and beliefs."

"Networking is a great opportunity on the road to wealth, your net worth will be a reflection of your network."

"Learning to invest is more important than learning a profession. Professionals still work for money, while investors learn how to make money work for them. Most professionals work for entrepreneurs and investors."

"One of the reasons people live in poverty is they are uneducated financially, and never make attempts to build their own business."

"When you realize that trading hours for dollars is a big mistake you start to become financially educated. Working long hours in corporate America rarely allows you to obtain financial freedom, yet schools has always taught us that we should study hard, earn a degree, find a high paying job, and work hard. This philosophy leads to a lifetime of financial dependence, and years of laboring only to make someone else very wealthy. They do not teach you how to make money and build a significant net worth in college. You have two choices in life: you can choose to be your own boss and make your money work for you, or you can choose to allow companies to exploit your true value."

SPEAKING THE MONEY LANGUAGE

What is a financial statement? "Your financial statement is your life financially on paper, these statements are what financial institutions want to see when you go to them for any reason, such as: business ventures, lines of credit, or asking for loans. They want proof of your income, your expenses, your liabilities, and what assets you have.

THIS IS WHAT A FINANCIAL STATEMENT LOOKS LIKE

Income Statement

Income
Expense

Balance Sheet

Assets	Liability

INCOME: is the amount of money that is coming into you each month.

EXPENSES: is the money that is going out each month through bills.

ASSETS: are businesses, or real estate that you own, stocks that you have put money into, bonds that you have bought. Assets bring in money without you working for it.

LIABILITIES: are your debts, such as car loans, credit cards, mortgage payment, etc.

Financial education will teach you how to read these statements and use them to your advantage. Assets are what the rich use to build massive wealth.

Financial statements are a very important part of your business plan. Financial statements let you know how much money is coming in from assets, or any other income areas. They also let you know how much is going out through bills, and how much is left over on a monthly basis. Monitoring these statements daily gives you total control of your financial status, which is needed to remain competitive in the global market.

Financial statements let you know what is working, what is not working. What is making money and what is not making money. They allow you to cut off the things that are not making money, before they get out of control. These are great tools for you to use when building wealth.

Jonathan Wainwright

CRACKING THE CODE 101

UNDERSTANDING FINANCIAL STATEMENTS IS THE KEY TO BUILDING WEALTH, AND HELP YOU LEARN THE LANGUAGE OF MONEY

"The dictionary defines financial statement as: written record of the financial status of an individual, or business."

"Due to a lack of financial education in schools, most people do not know how to read or understand financial statements."

"These statements tell you the financial facts of your business and your personal life. They also tell you if you are going up or going down on your journey to wealth."

"Financial Statements are the eyes, ears, and mouth to your business. They see, hear, and tell you everything that is going on financially inside your business, and personal life."

"Knowing the financial status of your business on a daily basis, gives you an advantage in the business world. When you know what is working, and what is not working. When you know how much money is going out and how much money is coming in, you become more accurate in your decision making, and can better capitalize on the growth of your company."

FINANCIAL RESPONSIBILITY

It is impossible to draw a blueprint of your new financial

direction and/or destination, which should be amongst the ranks of the millionaire, billionaire, trillionaire club, without knowing where you are financially RIGHT NOW!

In other words, how do you know where you are going, if you do not know where you are? It takes twice as long to get to the North pole when you are traveling south. You have to know where you are right now, to start heading in the right direction so you can reach your desired destination, the millionaire, billionaire, trillionaire status.

Now, start by opening up all your financial statements, credit reports, debt obligations, such as home payments, car payments, or any other outstanding debts. It is only when all of these documents are on the table for viewing can you set priorities and calculate your next step which should be credit restoration, with advancing credit scores, that will make banks and other financial institutions ready and willing to do business with you.

It is your financial responsibility to become financially successful, nobody else will do it for you. Wealth is something no one is willing to just throw your way, you have to go out and earn it for yourself. If you are waiting for someone else to hand you success, then wealth is not for you. Remember that most people in this world are financially illiterate and know almost nothing about money. The person that is aiming to become rich must take full responsibility over their financial elevation.

CRACKING THE CODE 101

BANKS LOAN MONEY TO PEOPLE WHO KNOW HOW TO USE MONEY TO MAKE PROFITS, HOW TO READ FINANCIAL STATEMENTS, AND KNOW THE IMPORTANCE OF CREDIT. YOU HAVE TO MAKE BANKS AND OTHER FINANCIAL INSTITUTIONS READY AND EAGER TO DO BUSINESS WITH YOU.

"You have a financial responsibility to find out your financial status, credit status, debt obligations and any outstanding financial debt.

"Banks and other financial institution love people that are financially responsible, know how to handle debt, and how to use debt to create wealth."

"You have a financial responsibility to gain a financial education, to ensure you travel the roads of prosperity and wealth, and not end up in the land of poverty."

"Knowing where you stand financially is a head start in the pursuit of riches. Your next step should be learning how to use your financial status to get ahead in life."

"Learning to use debt and OPM is your responsibility, and a major key on the road to success and financial freedom."

O. P. M. / DEBT

The definition of OPM is: "Other people's money." Some people call it debt, but the whole concept is learning how to use other people's money to make yourself rich. This is one of the biggest secrets of the wealthy. The first trillion-dollar U.S.

based company (Apple), still utilize the secret of OPM, even after making trillions in revenue, they still borrow money and utilize debt. In fact it is one of their most profitable ideas, because debt is tax free!

Every smart businessperson, entrepreneur, and investors use OPM to make themselves very rich. If I borrowed $100,000 from Lighthouse Bank, then invested in a business that profited $75,000 a year, I could pay the bank $25,000 each year, and put $50,000 in my pocket each year. After four years, the bank would be paid in full, and I would profit $200,000 over the four years. Now the business profit is 100% mine, I have just created wealth for myself with OPM I did not invest one dime of my own money. This one example could make me a millionaire. Imagine this on a much larger scale, you could do the same thing with five different businesses at the same time, and make millions of dollars.

Financially educated people understand credit plays a major part in this formality, so you must establish your credit, so banks and other financial institutions will be willing to do business with you.

> "Knowing how to use other people's money has always been a guarded secret of the very wealthy, if your focus is to become rich, you must learn what it is that the rich do. OPM is first on the list, but you have to know how to use it to become financially successful."

> "OPM is the gateway to financial freedom. Most of the world is not financially educated and do not have a clue how OPM could make them very rich. You must become educated on how to use OPM"

> "If someone loaned you one million dollars, would you

be broke in the next five years? Or, would you be able to add ten million to that one million. Rich people know how to use other people money to make themselves even richer, and you could learn the same thing."

CRACKING THE CODE 101

YOU HAVE TO BECOME A MASTER IN THE OPERATION OF OPM, IT IS THE KEY TO GENERATING WEALTH, IT WORKS BEST WHEN YOU KNOW HOW TO USE IT. LEARNING TO USE OPM HAS ALWAYS BEEN A SECRET OF THE RICH.

"Great wealth is founded on the use of debt, there is good debt and there is bad debt."

"If you borrow money and spend it on something that goes up in value, and has a positive cash flow, this is good debt. If you borrow money and spend it on something that will go down in value with a negative cash flow, this is bad debt. Using debt can make you extremely wealthy, if you know how to properly use it."

"Who will loan you money? The simple answer is: Banks, Hard Money Lenders, Private Investors, Pension Funds, any financial institution in the world. If you have great ideas, and in good standing with the credit bureaus, have great business plans, or assets, and recent financial statements, money will be chasing you."

"Most people buy real estate with none of their own money, strictly with the banks' money or private investors, and become very wealthy. You cannot use debt for liabilities, you must use debt to purchase cash producing assets. OPM is the key to wealth."

"Using debt in the form of credit card to buy clothes, shoes, personal vehicles, groceries, restaurant bills is bad debt. It is not bringing you back any money, nor is it producing anything of value, so it becomes a negative with interest."

LUXURY ITEMS

My friend wanted a sailboat for him and his wife, but he understood he could not afford one. One day, someone talked him into going inside a sailboat dealership just to check out the latest models and current prices. Once inside he could not believe all the new technology that had been added to the sailboat world.

After talking to one of the representatives at the dealership, he learned that these boats could be purchased with a reasonable down payment and monthly payments. My friend thought of a plan of how to buy one of these sailboats without using his own money. (which he did not have).

After going home and drawing up the blueprint to become the owner of a new sailboat, his blueprint stated that he would post online advertisements of a seven day and seven-night sailboat rental for $3,000. Which was the exact down payment of the sailboat he wanted. After many people wanted the seven day and seven-night cruise, and made their advance payments, my friend was in business. He rented out the sailboat for nine months out of every year, which covered the monthly payments and maintenance on the sailboat, plus a profit of positive cash flow in his pockets. He and his wife enjoyed the sailboat for the remaining three months of every year, absolutely free! His idea worked so well, the following year, he did the same thing with a private jet.

CRACKING THE CODE 101

LEARNING TO USE THE MIND AND YOUR THOUGHT PROCESS ALLOWS YOU TO CAPITALIZE ON THE USE OF OPM. ANYTHING THE MIND CAN CONCEIVE CAN BE ACHIEVED, KNOWLEDGE IS THE NEW MONEY

"The way you think is who you become. It is impossible to do extraordinary things when you are thinking ordinary thoughts."

"Buying luxury items with OPM is creative thinking, one reason people succeed is they have knowledge that other people do not have. The knowledge of OPM has always been a close kept secret of the rich."[2]

"You have a right to be rich, wealth starts in the mind. You were born rich, all you have to do is withdraw it from the mind through creative thinking."

"You must learn to make money from ideas, new ways of thinking gives you new ideas. You cannot expect to be rich when you have a poor thought process."

BONUS SECTION

BONUS 101

One needs to focus on acquiring assets, not income. Why? If you focus on income that means you have to keep working forever, focusing on assets means the assets are working for you forever. Business, real estate, stocks, bonds, and commodities are assets.

BONUS 102

Whatever you focus on always expand, you must learn how to receive information and process it into knowledge. You need financial education to know the difference between an asset and a liability, taxes are designed to help business owners, entrepreneurs and investors, in most cases they end up paying zero in taxes. Now ask yourself: How does a millionaire end up paying less taxes than someone that works at McDonald's? The answer is: financial education.

BONUS 103

The United States of America is a corporation that is over one hundred trillion dollars in debt. People with financial education do not work for paychecks, or enter into a 30-year mortgage for some house they may never own, giving your hard-earned money to stockbrokers, and corrupt financial adviser, is INSANITY!

HOW DO BANKS MAKE MONEY

Banks operate on something called the fractional reserve system. It works like this: If you deposit $100 into your saving account, the bank can now loan a qualified person $1000, at a high interest rate, using your $100 as the collateral.

To loan out a much higher fraction of your money, the bank is operating under something called "magic money." They are creating money out of thin air, so they need people to come and borrow money from them, most of the time the fractional reserve system is much higher, such as, when you put $100 in your savings account, the bank can loan out as much as $4000 at high interest rates, but to make all this work, they need qualified borrowers, and this is how the rich become richer, because they borrow the money the bank is begging to loan and buy assets that make them money. So basically, the asset repays the bank's loan, and make the borrower rich, because the asset is also putting money in the borrower's pocket, and the borrower end up owning the asset. This is especially true with real estate. These should be your thoughts and views of entering the financial world.

CRACKING THE CODE 101

THE BANK IS NOT DOING YOU A FAVOR BY LOANING YOU MONEY, YOU ARE DOING THE BANK A FAVOR BY BORROWING THEIR MONEY WITH INTEREST, LEARN TO MANAGE DEBT TO ACHIEVE WEALTH

"Once a bank or any financial institution know you have experience in handling debt (OPM) and a successful payment history, they will loan you as much as you can handle."

"Banks are begging for qualified people to loan money, you have a financial responsibility to make sure you are that qualified person."

"The fractional reserve system make banks the master of OPM, these same banks need you to borrow their money so they can make a profit. Hopefully, after learning the knowledge contained in this book, you will become a master in the use of OPM, and wealth building."

"Learning to buy assets with OPM is real financial education and puts you on the road to massive wealth."

BUILDING THE MASTERMIND TEAM

All businesses have a financial team, but who are the team players? Different businesses require different team players, but these are the most common players:

* Certified Public Accountants (CPA)	* Advertisers
* Brokers	* Marketers
* Bankers	* Sales Reps
* Business Strategist	* Tax Specialist
* Managers	* Insurance Brokers
* Chief Executive Officers (CEO)	* Lawyers
* Chief Operating Officers	* Contractors
* Chief Financial Officers	* Engineers
* Architect	* Appraiser

You must assemble your own team according to the needs of your business. If you have great business ideas, most of these people will work for a partner percentage, which is a good strategy because now they have an interest in making your business grow. Organized efforts create wealth; organized effort is the coordination of two or more people acting at the same time with a common vision in the pursuit of wealth.

"Are you a specialist or a generalist?" A specialist is someone that knows a lot about a little, a generalist is someone that knows a little about a lot.

Example of a Specialist is: a Medical Doctor, lawyer, athletes, dentist, etc.. They know a lot about their profession, but they do not know much about anything else.

A Generalist knows a little about everything, they know in what capacity a doctor can operate, they know the complete duty of any lawyer, they also know the functions of a dentist. Specialist usually work for generalist. Generalist are business minded people, they set up hospitals for doctors, or Clinics for Dentist, start law firms and hire lawyers. A generalist knows how to build a team of specialist, CPAs, brokers, strategist, bankers and have them work together for one common goal that will benefit the whole team.

CRACKING THE CODE 101

CREATING A MASTERMIND TEAM IS TRUE FINANCIAL EDUCATION, AND HAS ALWAYS BEEN A ROAD MAP TO RICHES AND USED BY SMART WEALTHY PEOPLE. THIS IS A VERY VALUABLE SKILL THAT IS USED BY GENERALIST YOU MUST LEARN HOW TO EMPLOY SPECIALIST.

"It is a known fact that a group of people will produce more energy and more ideas then a single person. The global market needs energy and ideas which ultimately translate into money."

"Human being can mentally see the thoughts of those who we associate with, money minds think alike."

"With so many specialists under one roof, you as a generalist has just created a fail proof business."

"Learning to employ specialist is real financial education, and comes with many tax breaks and tax incentives."

"Assembling a winning team is a skill you must learn. Knowing which players are needed in each business that you build, is very important knowledge."

"Economic advantages may be created by anyone that surrounds themselves with a mastermind team. In this financial game of life, are you sitting on the sidelines, or are you actually in the game? In reality, this is a game you cannot afford to lose so play to win!"

CERTIFIED PUBLIC ACCOUNTANT

Certified Public Accountant, ("CPA") are a must in the business world. Entrepreneurs and investors must keep CPAs in their front pocket, accessible at all times. Knowledgeable CPAs are very valuable to your business, after all, they set the stage to the financial record keeping process. Meaning: they know how much cash is flowing in and out of your business, they are supposed to let you know if you are over budget, or under budget in a timely manner, so you can make quick adjustments to ensure profits. CPAs must also be tax experts, guiding you on how to use taxes to expand your business and pay as little as possible, hopefully zero. Tax avoidance is legal using creative taxes, but tax evading is very illegal, and could lead to jail. So a good knowledgeable CPA is worth their weight in gold.

CRACKING THE CODE 101

ALL CPAs 'ACCOUNTANTS' ARE NOT EQUAL, HOWEVER, THEY ARE VERY IMPORTANT TO YOUR BUSINESS. YOU MUST FIND A VERY SMART AND KNOWLEDGEABLE CPA

"Certified Public Accountants are very valuable in building your business, they must know about creative taxes, meaning they have to know how to avoid taxes not evade them."

"General Electric made two billion in profits and paid

zero in taxes. Now you see how valuable a very smart CPA can be when it comes down to taxes, but that is not the only area your CPA should be knowledgeable in, cash flowing in and out is another area."

"If you had to donate money to charity because of a tax reason, a good CPA would have you and your family set up a 'Foundation' designated to donating to charities that directly benefit you and your family."

"There is a lot of information you need to know about CPA and taxes. You must be able to understand the functions and duties of a CPA, because they can steal your money or your company's money without your knowledge."

PRINTING MONEY

Governments print money, which is called 'Quantitative Easing' (QE) in hopes of stopping the biggest markets from crashing and fund major financial institutions from falling on their faces. They also print money to fund very large production industries, hoping to keep employment rates high. However, while they are printing trillions of dollars; the money that already exists starts to lose its value because, now there is too much money in circulation. Which equals too much money chasing a small amount of products, causing the item that use to cost $5, to now cost $7, because the dollar bill becomes weak, and is now only worth $0.70. So if your money is just sitting in the bank, then everyday it is losing its value, which is called: 'parking your money. Never park your money, make your money earn more money instead of letting it lose value through QE and inflation.

CRACKING THE CODE 101

NEVER PARK YOUR MONEY! MONEY IS LIKE A MAGNET, IT ATTRACTS MORE TO ITSELF, THROUGH FINANCIAL EDUCATION YOU LEARN HOW TO MAKE YOUR MONEY WORK FOR YOUR OWN FINANCIAL GAIN.

"Why save money when governments are printing money day and night, put that money to work, so it can make even more money. Money just sitting in the bank is getting ate up by inflation."

"The government is printing money non-stop, I am not telling you to spend your money foolishly, but what I am telling you is: Invest your money in sound and secure investments."

"If you put your money in the bank, the bank will invest your money and will not give you a dime of the profits. Why not do that for yourself? This is the secrets of the rich, they keep their money working for them."

"The difference between the rich and the poor is financial education. Anybody can be rich, because anybody can gain financial education. The only thing standing in the way of you obtaining massive amounts of wealth, is 'YOU!'"

BONUS SECTION

BONUS 101

You have to learn how to control the cash flowing in, and most importantly control the cash flowing out. 'Cash flow' is the life blood of any business. When cash flows in, it must be appropriated masterfully, and when cash flows out it must be according to the company's budget. Overspending or under spending can cripple any business. Acquiring the knowledge of business management will be very helpful. Hiring a very bright CPA is also a great resource.

BONUS 102

Due to the lack of financial education in school, most people do not know how to make money unless they are working for somebody else. The owner of the company will not tell you how to make money outside of working for the company.

BONUS 103

Most people were born thinking of themselves as victims, quick to point the finger at governments, other wealthy people, and circumstances as their reason for not being rich. However, in today's world, especially in America, anybody can be rich. The only thing that is holding you back from being rich is: "YOU," and your way of thinking!

LEARN HOW TO BE A CAPITALIST

The word capitalist means: individuals or firms that are free to compete with others for their own economic gain. The profit motive is basic to economic life. Capitalists are business owners, entrepreneurs or investors. These people know they are free to pursue economic gain for themselves; they know how to build businesses; how to own businesses, and; how to invest so they might become financially free. One cannot live life to its full potential, unless one is financially free.

Becoming financially free is not hard, most people that are financially free did not attend college. They gained their knowledge through seminars, self-education, and real-life skills. Traditional education is for people that want to become employees. Capitalist become employers, and investors in pursuit of real financial success.

CRACKING THE CODE 101

CAPITALIST LEARN HOW TO CAPITALIZE AND BECOME SMART MONEY THINKERS; ALL RICH PEOPLE ARE CAPITALIST.

"Do you want to work for other people, or do you want people to work for you? Smart people become capitalist and then become your boss."

"Most people focus on being a democrat or republican. In reality both democrats and republicans are capitalist because America is a capitalist country and they are the representatives of the American Corporation."

"Capitalist is that 10% of the people in the world that make 90% of the money in the world. Learn to be a smart money thinker and join the millionaire, billionaire, trillionaire club."

"When you walk into any business and spend your hard-earned money, you should know that a capitalist is profiting off of you. Capitalists are rich because they manufacture the goods and services you pay for."

"Most capitalist are also generalist. They are money minded, business orientated, and very knowledgeable people."

"Capitalists have the knowledge of free enterprise, which means you are free to operate in the business world to get yourself rich."

"Capitalists know how to use OPM to make themselves wealthy. They know the value of certified public accountants, but most of all they know everything that an accountant should do and what an accountant cannot do."

"Learning to be a capitalist is very important. They know all the secrets of the rich and they use those methods everyday to gain massive wealth, and know how to speak the money language."

INVESTMENTS ONLY FOR THE WEALTHY

In the business world there are investments strictly for the wealthy, and then there are investments for everyone else. Investments are considered assets because they produce cashflow, this is the reason you must build businesses, to purchase assets! Employees cannot purchase cashflow assets, their budget will only allow them to purchase skeptical retirement plans that can only be accessed, without a penalty, when you are in your sixties. If you work for money, after taxes you will not have enough left over to purchase cash producing assets. Building businesses is your gateway to buying cash producing assets, buying assets is having your money work for you, learning to invest is learning to build a financial plan of action. The whole world has plans in their thought process to become wealthy, but only the ones that add actions to their plans actually become wealthy.

Employees cannot afford primary wealth, which is productive land, that will continuously produce large amounts of wealth, these type of investments are only for the wealthy, because the working class cannot afford them. You must learn to build businesses and purchase cash producing assets the same way the wealthy do.

CRACKING THE CODE 101

LEARNING TO INVEST IS VERY IMPORTANT. YOU CAN NOT WORK FOR MONEY IF YOU WANT TO BECOME WEALTHY, LEARN TO FOLLOW THE SECRETS OF THE WEALTHY, INVESTING IN CASH PRODUCING ASSETS IS FIRST ON THE LIST.

"Many people think investing is risky, and it can be; to financially uneducated people. Your greatest investment should be in financially educating yourself."

"Owning assets of primary wealth is the ultimate goal in all financial markets, all markets in the world depend on primary wealth holders, employees must learn to build businesses and become investors in this new information age."

"Working for money is the old industrial age way of thinking. In today's world purchasing cash producing assets is the knowledge that is needed to become wealthy. You must learn to capitalize on the same knowledge that the wealthy are using."

"The most valuable investments can only be invested in by accredited investors, which is an individual with $200,000 or more in annual income, or over $300,000 or more in annual income as a couple, or $1 million or more in net worth."

"The Securities and Exchange Commission (SEC) is the police of the investment world, they are required to protect the average investor from some of the worst or risky investments, in the same token they stop the average investor from entering the most profitable investment in the world."

GLOBAL MARKETS

You must educate yourself about the global marketplace, because opportunity is everywhere: China has over a billion people; So does India. Both of these markets could work to your advantage, whether it is the low cost of labor, learning to utilizing the manufacturing arm of these nations, or building businesses in these countries. Fast food franchise, have been big money makers in both countries. Africa is another very rich marketplace. Billionaires are being made everyday in the global market, it is as easy as finding out what certain countries need, then finding the countries that produce those items, and then putting the puzzle together for a profit! Elementary school kids could do this blindfolded, so why are you not taking advantage of the global market? There are so many countries to choose from. Everybody is buying and selling goods all over the world, and it can all be done from the comfort of your own home... **"Online!"**

CRACKING THE CODE 101

THE GLOBAL MARKETPLACE IS ONE OF THE FASTEST AND EASIEST WAY TO GET RICH, AND IT DOES NOT REQUIRE A COLLEGE DEGREE. WEALTHY PEOPLE ARE TAKING FULL ADVANTAGE OF THE GLOBAL MARKET YOU SHOULD TOO.

"The global market has trillions of dollars in transactions

everyday, most transactions are done over the internet."

"You can become wealthy fast in the global marketplace, connecting with overseas businesses will help you build your business faster, and make you more competitive in today's market."

"Half the world's population are together in China, India, and Africa. These countries are great customers for whatever products or services you are selling. They are also the manufacturing arms of the world."

"The global market has billions of customers at the click of a button, with the help of banks and other financial institutions, you could become wealthy using OPM to enter the global market."

"Global commerce is the lifeblood of todays civilized society. People from third-world countries are getting rich overnight in the global marketplace, and they have much less to offer than you. So, why are you just standing by watching the rest of the world get rich using the global market."

"Low wage countries could be a great benefit to you and your company. Whatever business you are in, the global market can enhance your profit, even if it is just white labeling, which is middle-maning deals and earning a profit.

THREE LEVELS OF WEALTH

In the world of wealth there are 3 levels of wealth, and the number one and most valuable is "primary wealth."

PRIMARY WEALTH: Holders are the ones that own the fertile land that has the Gold and Silver Mines on them, the land that has the oil under it. They own the territory where all the fish breed, and the land that is growing all the useful things that is needed in this life for survivals, primary wealth is resource wealth. These resources are needed to further human civilization.

CRACKING THE CODE 101

OWNING PRODUCTIVE LAND IS THE REAL WEALTH

SECONDARY WEALTH: is production wealth, production wealth holder are corporations who are farmers and factory owners that produce foods and other products. These corporations are paying the primary wealth holders so they may farm the land and get its resources to produce the food and make the products for the world market. The same is for oil companies, goldminers who mine the gold; fishermen who catch the fish; and the factory owners. They all must have agreements with the primary wealth holders. Therefore, secondary wealth holders are also millionaires, billionaires, and trillionaires.

CRACKING THE CODE 101

ENTREPRENEURS, CORPORATIONS AND FACTORY OWNERS ARE SECONDARY WEALTH HOLDERS, BUT EQUALLY IMPORTANT AS PRIMARY WEALTH HOLDERS

TERTIARY: When secondary wealth holders build companies and corporations, tertiary wealth holders invest in these companies and corporations through stocks and buying shares of the companies. Tertiary wealth holders are known as paper investors, they hold a "claim" to wealth, but not the wealth itself. The same goes for currency, paper money is not wealth. It is only a "claim" to wealth, tertiary wealth holders (shareholders) owns a claim to the secondary wealth holder's corporation, not the land on which the food is grown. Tertiary wealth holders are really stock market investors.

CRACKING THE CODE 101

STOCK MARKETS ARE VERY TRICKY AND CAN BE CONSIDERED GAMBLING, IF YOU WIN YOU MAY HAVE UNCOUNTABLE SUCCESS, IF YOU LOSE, YOU COLD JOIN THE RANKS OF THE HOMELESS. SO I RECOMMEND YOU INVEST IN YOUR OWN FACTORY OR MANUFACTURING PLANTS, TO BECOME A SECONDARY WEALTH HOLDER IF YOU CAN NOT BECOME A PRIMARY WEALTH HOLDER.

LEARN HOW TO ADD VALUE

Learning to add value means, finding a way to deliver the same type of service, or the same product to consumers for less money than they are currently spending, and make a profit at the same time. In other words, if you know someone that spends $10 a week on food, but only gets five items for the $10, your job would be to add value by finding a way to give that same customer those same five items for $8, or giving them 6 or 7 items for the same $10.

Adding value means doing more for less and still making profits. This style of business will make you rich overnight, and anyone can do it. A personal example: a construction company was searching for a roofing company to do all the roofs of a 50-unit housing development. All the roofing companies they spoke with wanted $2,000 for each roof, which totals $100,000 for the entire job.

I came along and offered to do each roof for $1,800, which totals $90,000. Which is $10,000 less than the others. Naturally, I won the contract, and I gave them the same quality of service for less money, and still made high profits.

CRACKING THE CODE 101

LEARNING TO ADD VALUE IS ONE OF THE FASTEST WAYS TO BECOME WEALTHY, DOING MORE FOR LESS IS THE KEY TO BIG BUSINESS, AND THE KEY TO MAJOR SUCCESS. THE WEALTHY HAS ALWAYS USE THE ADDING VALUE METHOD

"Learning to add value is a multi-million-dollar strategy, once you put this strategy in operations you will become a million-dollar player overnight, the global market is a great place for this strategy."

"You will knock your competition out of the water with the strategy of adding value, doing more for less and still making a profit."

"You must be able to turn your idea into action and opportunity, one great way to financial success is committing yourself to an inspiring cause that helps other people become financially successful."

"Prosperity flows from correct thinking, and learning to add value is thinking correctly which could transform your financial status from rag to riches."

BONUS SECTION

BONUS 101

You must be thirsty for knowledge everyday of your life. Learning is something you will do for the rest of your life, become a lifetime learner. Knowledge is one of the secrets of the rich, but knowledge is nothing more than learning how to do a certain thing. Anyone can do it, if you learn how to ride a bike, then you will have a working knowledge of riding bikes, it is just that simple. Find out what it is that you need to learn, then simply obtain the knowledge of it.

BONUS 102

Nobody knows everything. Never let pride block you from learning something you do not know, by acting as if you know everything. You will not exceed the limits that you have set for yourself, you must get off the road of lack and limitation; and get on the road to wealth and prosperity. You must learn to make money from ideas. New ways of thinking, gives you new ideas.

BONUS 103

You have to shift from being a consumer to becoming an owner. The secret to getting ahead is getting started, you have to be able to look at the bright side of a dark situation and be willing to create opportunities that will benefit others. Your real power is being able to turn ideas into assets.

TAXES BECOME PROFITS

The entire tax code was written to benefit business owners, entrepreneurs, investors, and the wealthy. It was not written for the benefit of employees, or self-employed people. The IRS became a treasure chest to business owners, entrepreneurs, and investors. In the same token, employees and self-employed people live in fear of the IRS.

The Tax-code punishes people that work for money, but the tax code rewards people that make money work for them. That is why all the rewards are going to business owners, entrepreneurs, and investors, because they have mastered the game of making money work for them.

You should follow the same blueprint and make your money work for you. Business owners, entrepreneurs and investors are making tons of money, buying more assets, building bigger business, and becoming billionaires while paying very little and in some cases "zero" in taxes.

Employees, and self-employed people, pay 40-60% of their income in taxes leaving very little for themselves. Taxes make employees and self-employed people even poorer, while business owner, entrepreneurs and investors are getting rich off taxes.

CRACKING THE CODE 101

BECOME A BUSINESS OWNER, ENTREPRENEUR AND INVESTOR AND TAKE ADVANTAGE OF ALL THE TAX BREAKS AND TAX INCENTIVES THAT MAKE THE RICH, RICHER.
MAKE THE IRS WORK FOR YOU.

"When you invest in oil drilling in the United States, solar energy, clean energy, affordable housing, agriculture, or manufacturing, just to name a few, the government will literally give you your money back over a period of time, you cannot lose."

"When you buy equipment or machinery that is needed to run your business, you can recoup your investment through taxes under depreciation, while you get to keep the equipment and machinery, which are considered assets. You also keep the profit those assets produce."

"Real estate is a great cash cow with great tax breaks and incentives, you receive depreciation, appreciation, plus phantom income. The government loves people that create affordable housing, you become rich from all these tax gifts."

"Tax write-offs are something the wealthy has been using since the beginning of the IRS. Every expense you have could be a potential write-off, such as, rent or mortgage payments, car payments, utilities, food bills, phone bills, travel expenses, and many more. Anything that can be considered a business expense. If you have an office at your home, every bill connected to that home is a potential tax write-off: the car you drive to your commercial office building, the rent and utilities at your commercial office building, traveling to meet your customers, taking customers out to dinner, anything dealing with you and your business is a write-off. Sorry! The people who work hard for someone else cannot use these tax write-offs; you have to be a business owner, investor or, entrepreneur."

"Employee's biggest single expense is taxes. You will pay more in taxes than you will spend on any other single item."

DIVERSIFY YOUR ASSESTS

You must be wise, and own and operate a different variety of asset classes, do not put all your money into the stock market, or the real estate market. Do not put all your funds into one business even if you own one hundred percent of the business, diversify your asset classes.

You must create a variety of assets that produce cashflow, if one market is down, the other markets will still be producing cashflow, "do not be confused" stocks, bonds, mutual funds, hedge funds are all paper assets, and all the same market.

There are four different basic asset markets: Business; Real Estate; Paper Assets, and; Commodities. The ideal thing to do is have assets and investments in each basic asset market.

CRACKING THE CODE 101

DIVERSIFY OR DIE! DIVERSIFY INTO ALL FOUR BASIC ASSET CLASSES, NOT JUST PAPER ASSETS BE SMART AND DO WHAT THE WEALTHY DO "DIVERSIFY!"

"Do not put all your money into paper assets because, when the market crashes - as it often does - you will not lose everything in one fall. Investing only in paper assets is not financial education or sound advice."

"You should know not to put all your eggs into one basket. If one market is down, you do not have to lose sleep because you were smart enough to diversify your assets."

"Most people think because they have mutual funds, hedge funds, stocks, and bonds that they are diversified, but in reality, they are all in the same asset class. If you invested all your funds in 'paper assets' and the stock market crashes, you will lose everything in that crash. Just so you know, wealthy people love when the stock market crashes."

"When markets crash people that are well diversified are safe from bankruptcy, other people that were not so smart are now looking for a job, because they were wiped out due to a lack of financial education."

BONUS SECTION

BONUS 101

No one is ever defeated until defeat has been accepted as reality. Most people are like a drowning man; they use up many times the energy that it would take to save them in an aimless struggle without thought, or direction, exhausting themselves while getting nowhere.

BONUS 102

Never give into the belief that two powers exist, GOD is the only power. There is no power or reality in evil, evil is only what you make it out to be, after you know this truth, only positive and prosperous things will happen in your life, people have said courage contains genius and magic. Face a situation fearlessly and in reality, there is no situation to face because it falls away of its own weight.

BONUS 103

Unforgiveness is the biggest cause of misery and pain. Learning to forgive means letting go of the things that are hurting you. When you hold on to situations of when people hurt you, betrayed you, or just flat out did you wrong; it is not hurting that person, it is only continuing to hurt you. Forgiving them and moving on will do more damage to them than holding on to what is hurting you.

PARTNERING UP WITH THE GOVERNMENT

The government wants to be your business partner. The government always partners up with investors and business owners. The government needs people that produce food, clean energy, oil, gas, solar power and jobs. If you become the creator or producer of any one of these areas, the government will reward you in many ways, the government is willing to share the risk with entrepreneurs through deprecation and tax incentives. People with real financial education understands this. They also understand the government has unlimited projects ready for outsourcing to anyone who can do the job, these are really road maps to riches that you need to take advantage of, remember knowledge does not apply itself, you have to take the first step.

CRACKING THE CODE 1 0 1

THIS IS ONE OF THE SECRETS OF THE WEALTHY "GOVERNMENT PARTNERSHIP" BECAUSE THE OPPORTUNITIES ARE UNLIMITED, BECOME A PART OF

THIS MONEY TRAIN RIGHT NOW!
HARD MONEY LENDERS

Hard money lenders are people who will give you a loan, when the banks are telling you "No!" They do not care about your credit, or your last car repossession, or unpaid parking tickets. All they care about is "what are you doing with the money" and "when will you pay the money back with interest." Usually they want to hold the deed, or title to whatever you are buying until the money is repaid. One example is someone wanted to buy a really nice dump truck, so he could start a business hauling material for companies that was building new roads, and removing hazardous material from work sites. The hard money lenders gave him the money, but they held onto the truck title until the money was paid back, and put a GPS inside the dump truck, but they gave him the money to start his business with no hassle. Hard money lenders are out to make money, so they will partner up with you, and provide the start up capital for your business plans, blueprints and great ideas.

CRACKING THE CODE 101

HARD MONEY LENDERS ARE EVERYWHERE AND EASY TO FIND READY TO PARTNER UP WITH YOU IN HOPES OF MAKING THEM A PROFIT

DUE DILIGENCE

Due Diligence is the investigative process of business, where you investigate or inspect businesses or people that you are considering doing business with, finding out all the details before finalizing a business deal, also called the fact-finding process, this help you make the decision of should you do business with this company or not. Due diligence is looking at a company payment history, such as late payments, non-payments, the reliability of the company "will this company deliver on time, the credit rating, and the company ability to fulfill your company needs effectively. So make sure you do your due diligence.

CRACKING THE CODE 101

DUE DILIGENCE IS A MUST, THIS IS YOUR CHANCE TO LOOK AT A COMPANY FINANCIAL STATEMENTS AND VIEW THEIR PROFORMANCE BEFORE SIGNING A CONTRACT WITH THAT COMPANY

THE GOVERNMENT

The government does not know how to make money, all they know how to do is spend money, that is why they collect taxes they collect almost 35-40% every paycheck from hard working Americans, and almost 60-65% from self-employed workers. That is why smart people do not work for money, they learn to make money work for them and end up paying very little, in most cases "zero."

So if you are sitting around waiting on the government to take care of you, then you are planning on living a life of begging for money, social security is broke, Medicare is broke, the government is trillions of dollars in debt. Our government leaders could use some financial education. If you want to live the life GOD created you to live, you have to become financially independent by learning the truth about money through entrepreneurship and investing.

CRACKING THE CODE 101

GOVERNMENTS ARE CORRUPT YOU CAN NOT DEPEND ON THEM FOR FINANCIAL HELP, YOU MUST BECOME YOUR OWN BREADWINNER THROUGH ENTREPRENEURSHIP AND INVESTING, YOU CAN PARTNER UP WITH THE GOVERNMENT AND MAKE YOURSELF VERY WEALTHY

BONUS SECTION

BONUS 101

Financial freedom is the ultimate goal of life, learning to use the mind is the only pathway to obtaining financial freedom. You must gain the money conscious and see money coming to you from every source and every direction, most people in the world is brain washed into believing they are just a bag of bones. When in reality you was created before the world existed.

BONUS 102

You must plan your work and work your plan (blueprint) all things are possible to the one who believe he can do it. Never concentrate on your financial distant, only concentrate on your financial direction. Working a job will make you a living, becoming a capitalist will make you a fortune. Everyone can become very wealthy, including you.

BONUS 103

Life is a cruel teacher. It punishes you first; then gives you the lesson. The best way to amass large amounts of wealth is to find people who have already achieved what you want to achieve and follow their path to success. You have to know which direction you are heading in "success or failure" because if you do not know where you are going; every road you travel will end up being a dead end. Make success your only option.

FINANCIAL EDUCATION

Most people that you ask, what is the most important factor in building wealth? All would say "Having a Great Job!!" You will be surprised how many people believe having "a great job" will make them rich. This is foolish thinking! Wealthy people do not work for money, they build businesses and buy other people's time and make a profit in the process. You must learn these same skills.

It is commonly known in today's world that having a great job, working hard, climbing the corporate ladder to more responsibility will eventually bring you wealth and happiness. The fact remains that a great job barely supports the necessities of life, such as: food; shelter; bills and; clothing. Wealth is when small efforts produce large results; whereas poverty is when large efforts produce small results.

How ambitious are you? Are you ambitious enough to make Five-Hundred Million dollars, or are you just ambitious enough to make Five-Hundred dollars? Most people do not have clarity about what they want, and knowing with your heart, body and soul what you want is the first level of obtaining wealth.

Why is it that money seems to chase some people, and run away from others? This question has always intrigued me. Now

I am determined to find the answer, after much research, I have discovered that people have different ways they think about money. 99% of the way you think about money comes from your background and upbringing. Most people grew up believing that: in order to become wealthy, you have to become greedy, selfish, cold hearted, or some type of crook. We were taught to believe that being poor was more acceptable than becoming wealthy. (It is easier for a camel to go through an eye of a needle, than for a wealthy person to enter heaven). You do not have to be filthy, to be filthy rich.

Many believe that in order for one person to become rich, another person has to become poor. Which is total nonsense! This is domesticated thinking, do not let this type of thinking prevent you from becoming wealthy.

The people or system that is teaching us that it is unethical to become financially successful are secretly doing exactly what they are telling you not to do! How did so many people get all this misinformation about wealth? The American education system. (Domesticated Teaching) Domesticated means you have been programmed to think in a certain way which leads to failure. Most people say they want to become wealthy so they can leave their kids financially secure. What they don't know is leaving your kids financially secure with no financial education is equal to throwing your money down a black hole. Money and financially uneducated people will part ways very fast. Why not educate them financially at the same time you are educating yourself. Kids are never too young to learn, they may even learn faster than you. So financially educating your kids could be your smartest investment.

You must start right now involving your kids in the wealth

building process, you have to make sure they do not get domesticated in the same way you were once programmed. Remember you have to utilize the same methods the rich use, and one of the main things the rich do is set up corporations for their children and show them how to run them, at young ages.

Money comes from financial education. With traditional education, one would struggle to make a living; with financial education you will easily make a fortune. Most people think they have money problems, but in reality, their problems come from a 'lack of financial education.' Your success comes from your financial education, not from how hard you work. When you think about the wealthiest people in the world, they became wealthy because of the financial knowledge they gained, you can do the same thing!

Most people that are struggling, see themselves as not having enough money, but the truth is; their struggle comes from not having enough financial education. Learning is not hard or difficult, learning is something you do naturally when you apply yourself to any process.

Learning becomes fun and exciting when you can immediately put what you learned to work for a profit. Building wealth is a matter of learning and applying yourself, anyone can become wealthy. If you learn the necessary financial knowledge, money will be chasing you! Then you would really have a money problem, which would be finding a way to spend it. Once you become financially educated, and you start to use this education for financial gain, you will understand that money flows according to your level of education and your understanding of it. When I say: "You must learn the secret of the rich" or "you must do as the wealthy do." What I mean is:

"wealthy people have already made it to where you are trying to go. Why not follow the blueprint they have already built."

In reality, they are following someone else's blueprint, someone that did it before them. Wealthy people are standing by and wondering why other people are not following the money train. They understand the blueprint does not belong to any one person, everyone can use it. So, why not you?

I am always hungry for useful knowledge because I realize there is so much I do not know. I am not an expert and never want to be. Experts believe they have no room for growth, and claim to have all the answers. The business world is forever moving forward, so you must keep learning. What you learn today will be obsolete tomorrow. This is the reason learning is so important.

Wealthy people continually attend seminars gaining more education and chasing the newest cutting-edge information. Becoming wealthy is fun and exciting. All you have to do is apply yourself to learning the secrets the wealthy use. They are human beings just like you, except they apply the financial knowledge they have learned. Most people just dream and wish for wealth but are unwilling to dedicate time to learning how to make their dreams and wishes come true. Remember, there are many different types of education.

Page 100 missing

your thought process transmits your thought energy to the mind in the form of your written goals, the mind without hesitation, uses people, places, and things to make those written goals show up in your life. Now you understand the importance of writing down all of your goals, dreams and ideas.

ACTION

The main reason people fail, when it comes to obtaining wealth is they have no action about themselves. Perhaps they feel they are not ready for success, they feel unprepared, disorganized, unsure, or afraid. If you try and fail, you can learn from your mistake, and continue on the road to wealth, but if you fail to try, you could become one of the biggest losers of all times.

Action is the main ingredient in success. Without action, you will never accomplish anything of value. The person that is not afraid to take action will be the one to enjoy great success. Never be afraid of success, when you believe you are unprepared, unsure, or just not ready, you are actually telling yourself that you are afraid of success. Remember this train of thought comes from being domesticated, there is no reason in the world that you should be afraid of yourself.

MONEY MANAGEMENT

Money management is also a main ingredient in wealth building, remember the old proverb "A fool and money are soon parted." Is there any truth to this old proverb? The answer is: "Yes!" A fool does not know how to manage money.

Banks look for money management skills in entrepreneurs. If you have plans to become rich, money management is very important on the road to wealth. Certified Public Accountants (CPA) are great tools if you are having money management problems or concerns.

The world will rob you blind if you do not know how to manage your money, that is a sign of financial weakness. Learning to manage money is learning the difference between a liability and an asset. Knowing the meaning of words like, equity, depreciation, appreciation, leverage and OPM, puts you ahead of the game in financial circles. Once your money management skills are improved, your financial status will also improve.

My goal is to teach you the importance of money management, you will not succeed until you have conquered that area on the road to riches.

GETTING PREPARED

How do you expect to win if you are not prepared? Preparation is very important in the world of money. Preparing usually means doing all the things most people do not like to do. It means studying and learning; It means reading books and going to seminars; It means not being afraid of success, and ready to take action; It means having your personal and business credit in tip-top condition; It means having your bankers, investor, transactional funding, CPA, Lawyer, co-signers, buyers, sellers and contacts on standby, waiting on you to enter the arena.

You must be ready to research and investigate every deal that passes through your hands. You have to know where to get the answers to questions you have no knowledge of. We are entrepreneurs and investors, not experts, so you have to realize you do not know everything, but you must be smart enough to know where to find the answer.

Are you really prepared? If not, now is the time to put on your hard hat, and get your thought process working. Time to jump on the highway to wealth.

CRACKING THE MILLIONAIRE CODE

PART IV

MONEY TALK

MONEY TALK

Other People's Money is debt. Money borrowed by individuals or companies looking to gain financial leverage, or looking to expand existing companies in hopes of creating even greater wealth. OPM is considered an asset to companies if used correctly because of its potential. A key factor to wealth is learning how to use OPM.

MONEY TALK

Finance Company are companies that are engaged in making loans to individuals and businesses. Unlike banks, finance companies do not receive deposits. Most finance companies accept individuals with low credit scores, and work with almost any company that does not qualify for bank loans. Finance companies have higher interest rates than banks.

MONEY TALK

Commodities are bulk goods that are sold all over the world, but primarily through the 'Commodity Index' of every major trading market in the world. The major commodity categories are: energy, crude oil, heating oil, natural gas, agriculture, livestock, metals, coffee, cocoa, sugar, orange juice, and cotton. Commodities are one of the biggest markets in the world.

MONEY TALK

Return on Investment (ROI) is profit made from an investment only after the original invested money has been returned. Everything after that is the return on your investment, unlike capital gain, where you buy low and sell high for a one time profit. In most cases ROI is cash flow, meaning after receiving your initial money back, the profit flows in for years, Sometimes forever!

MONEY TALK

Profits are positive differences resulting from selling products and services for more than the cost of producing the products or services.

MONEY TALK

Proceeds are the money received from any transaction after all deductions have been taken out. Example: XYZ Manufacture sells its cookware sets through multiple distribution channels, such as: brokers, wholesalers, and bargain plus internet websites, who all operate for a profit. When the cookware sets are sold through one of the links above, after getting their commission off the sale, the remaining money goes to XYZ. The money that remains is the "Proceeds."

MONEY TALK

Factoring Companies are financial services that purchase account receivables from companies. Example: XYZ Manufacture has 300 customers that are making monthly payments to XYZ for cookware sets that was sold to them on credit, which is called "account receivables" and factoring companies will buy these accounts from XYZ for a smaller amount than what the customer actually owes. Since the factoring company paid XYZ the smaller amount up front, when the factoring company collects the full payment from the 300 customers it makes a profit in the process.

MONEY TALK

Account Receivable is money owed to a business for merchandise or services that was sold on credit, it is also known as 'Open Accounts.' Example: XYZ Manufacture has 300 customers that are making monthly payments for cookware sets that was sold on credit, they created open accounts that are due monthly, which are referred to as account receivables.

MONEY TALK

Account Payable is money your company owes to other companies for goods or services that were extended for payments. This is the opposite of accounts receivable.

MONEY TALK

Elephants are large financial institutional investors, which are banks, pension funds, mutual funds, hedge funds and insurance companies, who have billions or trillions of dollars in assets, cash, stocks and bonds. These elephants move their investments around in a herd like manner causing markets to rise very fast, or plunge downward in seconds.

MONEY TALK

Tax Havens are countries offering outside businesses and individuals an environment with little or no taxation. Several Caribbean Islands, such as the Cayman Island have attracted people from all over the world that have deposited their money into these banks because of soft regulations, and increased privacy.

MONEY TALK

Purchase Orders (PO) are written authorizations to a vendor to deliver specified goods or services at a stipulated price. once the PO is accepted by the vendor, it becomes a legally binding purchase contract.

MONEY TALK

Intellectual Property is intangible assets, things that you can not touch, such as ideas and knowledge. However, intellectual properties can be protected by copyrights, patents, or trademarks. Many corporations own intellectual property which puts them at an advantage in the marketplace.

MONEY TALK

Inflation means money not worth its initial value, such as; one dollar being only worth .90, because of inflation. This happens when governments print too much money (QE). It looks like the price of merchandise is going up, but really the value of the dollar is going down, so the dollar loses its purchasing power, creating a weak dollar. Example: XYZ Manufacture was getting 10 gallons of gas for 22 dollars, now because of inflation, XYZ is only getting 8 gallons of gas for the same $22.

MONEY TALK

Weak Dollar is when money has fallen in value and is not worth the number that is printed on the bill. This happens for many reasons; inflation (QE); large trade and budget deficits; unattractive interest rates, and; declining market trends. When the dollar is weak you are able to purchase less items.

MONEY TALK

Deficit means excessive debt and liability that is greater than your income and assets. Deficits are usually corrected by productivity, or the selling of assets. Excessive spending over the budget creates a deficit. The United States deficit including Social Security and Medicare is over one hundred trillion dollars in debt.(Unfunded Liabilities)

MONEY TALK

Earning Assets are money producing assets, such as real estate, rental property, equipment, business, etc... Example: XYZ

Manufacture invested money into machinery and equipment, so they could manufacture cookware sets. The machinery and equipment are earning assets because they produce products that translate into cash flow.

MONEY TALK

Recession is a downturn in economic growth activities, and a general decrease in business which leads to high unemployment rates. Money becomes tight, corporations start to collapse because the gross national product markets begins to crash. All financial institutions, such as investment banks, savings and loan companies, credit unions, insurance companies, brokerage firms, start to flop, because most of their capital is invested in these corporations that are downsizing, and have almost no productivity. A recession is economic death.

MONEY TALK

Dividend is monies paid out to shareholders from the corporations they invested in, dividends is the gain from their initial investment. Dividends are usually paid out quarterly from one or many distribution areas, such as capital gains or interest income. Dividends can be reinvested under (DRP) or rolled over for later payments.

MONEY TALK

Outsourcing is when one company contracts obligations to another company. Getting another company to do the work your company would otherwise be doing. Many U.S. companies outsource work to low wage countries. Example: XYZ Manufacture outsourced some of its manufacturing duties to China, because China is a low wage paying country. XYZ allows the Chinese companies to manufacture individual pieces of its cookware sets, then ship them to America to be assembled into the full cookware set. In the past, XYZ did all of its own manufacturing.

MONEY TALK

Tax Shelters are methods used by investors to legally avoid or reduce tax liabilities. Legal shelters include Individual Retirement Accounts (IRA), Life Insurance account, tax exempt municipal bonds, charitable contributions, anything that will help you legally avoid taxes that work towards your present and future benefit.

MONEY TALK

Shareholders are tertiary investors. They invest in other people's corporations by buying stocks in the company. Their investment allows them to have a claim to the corporation, but not ownership. Shareholders are investing for capital gains, such intentions are to make a return on their investment.

MONEY TALK

Home Equity Line of Credit (HELOC) is granted to a homeowner by a mortgage lender such as a bank, or credit union using the value of the homeowner equity as collateral, the interest cost of the loan is tax deductible. HELOC is very popular in the banking industry.

MONEY TALK

Debt is money owed. A person can be in debt personally and/or through a business. Basically, debt is borrowed money or bills such as: utilities, food bills, car notes, and many more. Debt can be lowered or erased by paying it off.

MONEY TALK

Before Tax Dollars is profits your company has made but has not yet paid taxes in hopes of tax avoidance. Example: XYZ Manufacture has made $300,000 off its cookware sets, but December 31 is approaching, which is year end tax season. XYZ Manufacture is also thinking of tax avoidance, so XYZ takes its 'before tax dollars' and spend the amount it would pay in taxes and buy more equipment and supplies to make more cookware sets, and pay all the company's bills. Under business expenses all these are write offs. XYZ Manufacture has just leveled its tax obligation to "zero" legally with "Before Tax Dollars."

MONEY TALK

Quantitative Easing (QE) means the government is printing money to prop up the economy in hopes of saving the largest financial markets and industries from crashing. The banking industry, the stock markets, the automobile industry, the real estate market, the wireless communication industry, and phone companies. All these markets and industries were failing, and most had already crashed, so the government started printing money (QE) in efforts to save these markets from totally collapsing. The government has printed over one hundred trillion dollars to help save the economy, even though it caused inflation.

MONEY TALK

Phantom Income is money that appears out of thin air, such as appreciation. Example: if you purchased a house last year for $100,000 and this year the market value went up. Now that same house is worth $125,000, you have a phantom income of $25,000 because it came out of thin air, something that was not there before. Tax avoidance is phantom income because that is money you would otherwise have to pay. Depreciation is also phantom income because the government gives you tax incentives in the form of write offs.

MONEY TALK

Capital Gains is money that has been made from investment, such as stocks, bonds, mutual funds, or any asset or item that is purchased at one price and sold at a higher price. The amount that was made over the buying price is capital gains. Example: if you purchased a table set for $25 and then sold it for $35, you have a capital gain of $10. Anytime you are buying low and selling high, you are investing for capital gains. Investing for cash flow is not the same as investing for capital gains.

MONEY TALK

Amortization means to reduce debt by payments. Example: if you owe the bank $1,000, and you make monthly payments of $50, you are amortizing your debt. Amortize also means to pay off, or paid in full.

MONEY TALK

Earned Income is money that employees and self-employed people work for and receive in the form of a paycheck. Example: when employees, or anybody that works for money add up the total amount at the end of the year, that total is called "Earned Income." It is usually calculated for tax purposes.

MONEY TALK

Tax Avoidance means to legally pay the least amount in taxes through creative taxes, depreciation, charitable contributions, tax shelters, corporate trusts and company expenses. Example: companies can spend money on equipment, build bigger factories, buy parts, or supplies, anything the company needs to expand, or be considered a business expense; those are all 'Tax Write-offs,' which is tax avoidance. Any bills or debt connected to your company are tax write-offs, you can legally avoid taxes through such means, but you cannot evade taxes. A sure way to end up in prison is tax evasion!

MONEY TALK

Business Manager is someone that handles your day to day business affairs and is responsible for giving you observational advice. Meaning; they tell you the things that they see that can be improved within your company. Business Managers should be resourceful, by knowing where to locate licenses and permits needed to start or operate any type of business. In large corporations there may be a different business manager in charge of departments within a corporation. Example: XYZ Manufacture company has an advertising department, a marketing department, a human resources department, each department has a different business manager.

MONEY TALK

White Labeling is becoming the middleman of a business transaction and receiving a profit. Example: XYZ Manufacture has several online stores that sells its own cookware sets, those same online stores sell products manufactured by other corporations, and receives a percentage of the profit off each sale.

MONEY TALK

Fun Money is money that is not necessary for everyday living expenses and can therefore be risked for investment purposes. If the investment pans out, the investor has had fun speculating; gained knowledge, and; made a profit. If the investment goes sour, the investor's lifestyle has not changed or been put at risk because he or she could afford to lose that money.

MONEY TALK

Enterprise Zone is geographical areas targeted by federal, state, or municipal governments where small businesses are given incentives to create employment opportunities. Incentives may include tax credits, favorable financing terms, contracts set aside, zoning regulation relief, or other types of help.

MONEY TALK

Equity is the amount that you own within any asset class of value. Example: if you buy a house from a bank for $100,000, and to this very day you have paid the bank $30,000, but still owe the bank $70,000. You have $30,000 in equity, and the bank has $70,000 in equity. Equity is your share, or percentage of ownership.

MONEY TALK

Depreciation means the monetary value of assets are going down in price. Example: the day you buy a new car and drive it off the showroom floor, it is no longer worth the amount you paid for it. Time and usage causes automobiles and other comparable assets to depreciate in value.

MONEY TALK

Holding Companies are also known as parent companies, or first level, these type of companies own lots of other companies, they are the headquarters of second level companies. Example: XYZ Manufacture is owned by the Jackpot Group. The Jackpot Group also owns ABC Manufacturing, and 123 Imports. Holding companies are great for tax consolidations, tax incentives, and write offs.

MONEY TALK

Liquidation means to sell assets for cash to pay debts or other obligations; and distributing the remaining assets and cash to the owner. Companies in bankruptcy are sometimes forced into liquidation.

MONEY TALK

Advance Payment is up front money that has not been earned yet. Companies give advance payments for goods and services that will be delivered in the near future, home contractors require advance payment from homeowner to buy building materials.

MONEY TALK

Interest Rates is additional money charged for the use of borrowed money. Example: XYZ borrowed $10,000 from the bank, not only does the bank want its original $10,000 back; the bank also wants an additional $1,300 through the interest rate, which is the cost of loaning XYZ Manufacture the $10,000. Therefore, total amount XYZ Manufacture repaid to the bank is $11,300.

MONEY TALK

Electronic Cash (E-cash) is digital money, computer technology that stores a coded credit/debit card number in the hard drive and permit purchases at websites without re-entering card information.

MONEY TALK

Escrow Account is money, securities, or property being held by a third party until the conditions of a contract, or agreement is final. Example: XYZ is doing business with an overseas supplier, but this is their first deal, so XYZ does not want to just hand over the payment without checking the quality of the product. As a solution, XYZ puts the payment in an escrow account. This means a third party (banks) or (lawyers) is holding the payment until XYZ inspects the product and then orders the release of the payment to the overseas suppliers.

MONEY TALK

Revolving Credit is credit extended to an individual or a company, where the total amount of credit extended is constantly available for use and the amount of credit that is in use is payable in monthly installments. Revolving credit is also known as 'revolving accounts' or 'revolving lines of credit.' Tradelines, or Trade Accounts are open credit accounts with vendors/suppliers of goods and services. Example: let's say you owned XYZ Manufacture and you manufactured cookware sets, and you shipped the cookware sets to your customers through Federal Express and UPS. Both companies will extend you revolving lines of credit, where you pay monthly premiums not the whole amount at one time, but you will pay the full amount over a period of time.

MONEY TALK

Net 30, 60 & 90 means when vendors extend you lines of credit, they expect to be paid in a specified time frame, either 30, 60, or 90 days. Example: If Federal Express and UPS extended you a line of credit with a Net 30, they expect full payment in 30 days. The same applies to Net 60 or 90. The vendor presumes the full amount will be paid in the specified time period.

MONEY TALK

Vendors are suppliers of goods and services, manufactures, importers or wholesale distributors, they issue out tradelines, which is open account or lines of credit to companies, which is called vendor accounts, it will be either a revolving account, or a net 30, 60 or 90. Example: UPS and Federal Express are vendors, who both are willing to handle your shipping needs and will extend you lines of credit.

MONEY TALK

Tradeline means the actual open account between the vendor and your company, you are trading money, products and services through lines of credit, which are tradelines.

MONEY TALK

Appreciation means assets going up in value. Example you brought your house for $100,000 last year, but this year it has went up in value to $120,000. Your house has appreciated $20,000.

MONEY TALK

Interest Earnings means the amount of money that have been profited from your money that is working for you. Example: you have $1,000 in the bank, and after one-year that $1,000 has accumulated interest. Say $75 has been added to your $1,000, this is the interest earning the bank is giving you for having your $1,000 sitting in their bank.

MONEY TALK

After Tax Dollars means income that has already been taxed by the government (IRS). Example: when employees receive their paycheck and the necessary deduction has already been taken out, such as: federal income tax, local and state taxes; the amount that is left is call after tax dollars.

MONEY TALK

Entity means organizations, corporations, or governments which has a legal identity separate from its members. Example: XYZ Manufacturing is a corporation, not a human being, it has its own identity. A corporation/entity cannot be owned, it can only be ran by directors and officers. Entities stand alone, but are financial vehicles that can be used by human beings to accomplish a collective task to gain financial success.

MONEY TALK

Flow Through means, profits and losses can flow straight through the entity directly to the owner's personal tax return, leaving the corporation with no tax obligation, which is now transferred to the individual owner.

CRACKING THE MILLIONAIRE CODE

PART V

BUSINESS AS USUAL

HOW TO SET UP A CORPORATION

The first step for 'S' or 'C' corporations are the "Articles of Incorporation" being filed with the Secretary of State, which are 3 simple pieces of paper. It is the same process with an 'LLC,' but different names. The LLC's documents are called "Articles of Organization." With a "LP" it is called "Certificate of Limited Partnership." All must be filed with the Secretary of State in whatever state you are incorporating.

Most corporations use lawyers or companies such as legalzoom.com, corporatenow.com or many others to set up their corporation, which cost between $99 and $800, depending on which company you use, after the necessary paperwork has been filed with the Secretary of State. The next step is to get an Employee Identification Number (EIN), go to irs.gov and they will assist you in obtaining your EIN with a quick questionnaire. Which concludes the process.

The best states to incorporate in is: Nevada or Wyoming; they have the best asset protection for your business. You do not have to live or do business in these states to incorporate there, most corporations in America was formed in one, or both of these states.

However, once you have incorporated in Nevada or Wyoming, and have your EIN in hand, it is time to pick which state you want to do business in. Let's say you decide to open your business in Florida. You must go to the Secretary of State in that state

(Florida) and register your Nevada, or Wyoming corporation to do business in Florida. Yes, you can register your Nevada or Wyoming corporation in multiple states at the same time.

Now that you are incorporated in Nevada or Wyoming, have your EIN and corporation registered in Florida with the Secretary of State. You must go down to the city or county licensing office in the city or county you wish to do business; apply for a business license for the type of business you want to operate. Which is very easy and inexpensive, in most states they require you to have a lease contract to the building where you plan to do business before you can register with them (a notice of occupancy may be required) A Post Office Box will work in most states for certain types of businesses. Each state has its own rules, but good attorneys can be helpful.

Now it is time to open a corporate account for your corporation. Remember, a corporation is not fully active, until a corporate account is attached to it. All this can be done in one day, you do not have to wait weeks.

DIFFERENT TYPES OF CORPORATIONS

In the business world today, you have many different types of corporations. The one you should use depends on the type of business you have. There is no special type of corporation for any special business, you have to use the one that makes more sense according to what you are trying to accomplish. Such as: flow through taxation; avoidance of employment taxes; or taking your company public.

Now, let's start with the Limited Liability Company (LLC); which is the most commonly known and used in America. LLC provides limited liability protection, which means the owners do not face personal liability for debt, or lawsuits that may come against the company. In other words: if the company is being sued and is found to be liable in a lawsuit; you as the owner cannot lose your personal assets. (i.e. home, cars, bank accounts or other businesses) As long as your personal asset is not directly connected to the LLC. The only thing should be owned by your LLC is whatever the business needs to operate effectively. DO NOT put your personal home, personal vehicles, personal bank accounts, or any other businesses at risk, whatever is owned by the LLC can be taken if your LLC is found liable in a lawsuit, unless there is a charging order procedure in place.

There are other features that make the LLC very unique, such as flexible management structure, and flexible allocation of profit and loss. A LLC may have one, or hundreds of owners, and an owner can be a single individual; a trust; another corporation; or a foreign citizen. LLCs also have flow through taxation. There are many options in structuring a LLC, so be sure to get with a professional when you structure your LLC, so it can be beneficial to you.

NEXT IS THE LP

A "Limited Partnership" (LP) is a different set up from an LLC. Limited Partnerships may have as many partners as you wish, but it has two separate classes of partners: General and Limited.

General Partners are responsible for managing the partnership, and holds the power in the partnership, general partners are held personally liable for all debts, and lawsuits brought against the company.

The Limited Partner is just that "Limited." They have no say in how the company operate, and they cannot be actively involved within the company, a limited partner is considered an owner, but has absolutely no power or input. However, another corporation, or LLC can be formed to serve as a general partner of a LP in hopes of limiting the liability of the general partner.

S CORPORATION

S-Corp is the entity of choice for small business, it can only have up to 100 shareholders, and they must be American Citizens or resident aliens, they cannot be corporations of any kind. S-Corp can only have one class of stock, (Preferred Stock) but it does have flow through taxation, and minimum self-employment taxes.

S-Corp also has flow through distribution, which means each shareholder gets paid the amount according to his/her percentage of ownership.

The sub-chapter S corporation, or S-Corp, was named after the IRS code section allowing it to exist.

C CORPORATION

C-Corporation are also known as "C-Corp," and is the only corporation that can be taken public. Many corporations start out as LLCs or S-Corps, but end up as C-Corp for the purpose of going public. Most C-Corporations are very big companies with millions of shareholders, and billions and in some cases Trillions of dollars in annual revenues. Which in most cases is the ultimate goal of corporations. One disadvantage of a C-Corp is double taxation. Once, when the C-Corp make a profit, it is taxed on the profit's gain. Then the shareholders are taxed once again when they received their dividends. The directors of these corporation are finding ways around the double taxation.

SOLE PROPRIETORSHIP

Sole Proprietorship, and general partnerships are not good entities, there are no protection with these entities, one lawsuit against your business, you could lose your house, savings, and all personal assets, including the shirt or your back.

WHAT IS A CHARGING ORDER?

Charging Orders are asset protection for LLCs and LPs only, other corporations cannot use this protection. If your LLC or LP is held to be liable in a lawsuit, a charging order can prevent them from taking everything inside your company. If your corporation is found guilty and you do not have a charging order, the person suing can take everything inside your company. All of your company's equipment, bank accounts, vehicles, they can literally "Take your Company." However, with a charging order in place, they cannot take ANYTHING. All they can do is wait until your company makes money and get a small amount of the company's profit. In most cases there are ways around even paying small amounts if you have a charging order and a good attorney.

WHY INCORPORATE IN NEVADA OR WYOMING?

These two states have the strongest charging order protection in the United States. They offer the best benefits for any corporation; you do not have to live or locate your business in these states for you to reap the benefits. Most companies in the United States are incorporated in Nevada, and Wyoming, but they are not located or doing business in those states, check with your attorney on how this works, charging orders are the best thing a corporation can have at its disposal.

BUSINESS CREDIBILITY CHECKLIST

* Business Name
* Business Address
* Business Entity
* EIN Number
* Local Phone Number
* 800 Number
* Professional Voicemail
* Fax Number
* 411 Listing
* Logo
* Website
* Professional Email
* Business License
* Business Permits

You can obtain all of the above in one day. There are thousands of companies that will set up some, or all of them for a fee; or you can do it all yourself.

MERCHANT ACCOUNT

If your business intends to accept debit and credit cards, you will need a merchant account. A merchant account allows your company to accept any type of payment instruments for products and services. All merchant accounts charge a fee, or percentage of the transaction for the flexibility of accepting card payments.

There are companies like square or clover, where you can accept debit and credit payments directly from your mobile device for a fee.

SOCIAL MEDIA BUSINESS

Social media has become a major aspect of the business world, it is not required but, it gives your business internet presence which is global presence.

Facebook   (www.facebook.com)
Linkedin   (www.linkedin.com)
Google+   (plus.google.com)
Tumblr   (www.tumblr.com)
Twitter   (twitter.com)
Instagram (www.intagram.com)
Snapchat   (www.snapchat.com)
Pinterest (www. interest.com)

CREATING YOUR WEBSITE

Your website has to have a unique address, called a URL or "domain name" that will be used on the server upon which it resides. Using the name of your business is your best choice, if another business is currently using the name you want; then you should pick the next closest name. Domain names must be registered for a minimum of two years, after which you can renew them. The cost to register a name for two years is approximately $70. There are many different companies that handle registration; www.godaddy.com and www.domain.com are the well-known sites.

After you have chosen your website name, now it is time to build your website. Companies such as: www.sitebuilder.com; www.web.com; or, www.weebly.com are very inexpensive web design solutions, in fact some are free. These companies offer templates for web design, domain name and webhosting. For instance: Weebly offers a basic templet for free, more complex sites cost a fee.

Now you have to choose a web host, you must choose a service to host your website. Examples of well-known web hosts are: Microsoft Network; Go Daddy, and Prodigy. However, there are many more smaller hosts available.

Now you have to promote your website, connecting to social media links, joining online discussion groups, columns in newspapers, trading web advertising with other websites, and telling friends and family, just to name a few. There are thousands of ways to promote your website.

Do not forget to keep fresh content and news on your site, the fastest way to run someone off your site is to have outdated

information, as you create your website, these are "Must Haves:"
* Home Page
* Contact Us page
* About Us page
* Testimonials from past clients and vendors
* Photos of whatever you are doing or selling
* Your company logo should appear on all of the pages

Having a website is necessary for any serious business, it has become a big part of doing business in the 21st century. You must have your site ready to do business with people anywhere in the world and ready to accept payments from most instruments.

Professional business must have valid phone numbers customers can call to talk to a real person instead of a complete automated system. Remember, in today's business world a majority of companies conduct their business online.

Customer service is a successful ingredient in running a profitable business. Businesses grow faster and run more smoothly when they listen to customer's feedback.

PERSONAL CREDIT

Personal credit is very important on your journey from rags to riches, and very easy to repair, using a few small steps you can wipe your slate clean. When applying for loans and credit, companies will look at your personal credit. Do not worry, below are the keys to credit restoration:

FIRST STEP: contact all three personal credit agencies Equifax.com; Transunion.com; Experian.com, annualcreditreport.com. Then request your FREE annual copy of your credit report. These reports will tell you names and addresses of any creditors that have placed derogatory accounts on your reports, which means companies have placed negative accounts on your credit report for non-payment.

STEP TWO: one way to resolve your debt/derogatory accounts is to dispute every derogatory account on those reports with each credit bureau. In most cases the companies you owe money will let you off the hook, or they may not have the proper paperwork showing that you actually owe them. (Most companies are not good at keeping accurate records) Those accounts will be dropped off of your credit report.

STEP THREE: The accounts that still remain; meaning the companies that have proved to the credit agencies that you do owe them, therefore, the information has been verified and confirmed and will remain on your report. You may set up a payment plan to settle the debt, which actually works in your favor, because you get a chance to show the banks and other financial institutions that you do pay your bills.

After you have completed all the above steps...

STEP FOUR: it is time to add tradelines and revolving accounts to your credit profile, these techniques are used to boost your credit score.

BUSINESS CREDIT

Business credit may be obtained once you open your own corporation. There are three major business credit reporting agencies, and various smaller ones in America. Dunn & Bradstreet, Experian Business, and Equafax Business are considered the top three.

D&B is used by most vendors who extend credit to

business, D&B is the largest of the three nationwide business credit reporting agencies. Once your business checklist is complete (see Page # 133) immediately contact all three business credit reporting agencies and put your corporation on the map by obtaining what is called a "Credit Profile Number" (CPN) D&B has it listed as a **"Dunns Number."**

Experian Business has it listed as a "Business Information Number."(BIN)
Equifax Business has it listed as a "EFX ID."

Once you have obtained your CPN from each business agency, you have now activated your business credit building process, any vendors you wish to do business with must use your CPN and report every transaction. In the first 24 months of being in business stay away from vendors that will not report to these agencies, most vendors will only report to these agencies if you default.

What you need to build your business credit is vendors that report monthly transactions, such as payment history and payment accuracy.

PERSONAL GUARANTEE

A personal guarantee is: You agreeing to personally take ownership and responsibility for a debt, or payment. Most banks and financial lenders want a personal guarantee from you for loans, corporations have a way of getting out of debt through bankruptcies or closing the corporation. However, with a 'Personal Guarantee' you are responsible no matter what happens. If you have a personal guarantee, and you default, financial lenders and banks can put a 'Lien' on your personal assets when personal guarantee loans are not payed back. In some cases, it can resort into criminal matters, depending on the circumstances.

ASSET PROTECTION

Insurance is the best asset protection for your business, home, vehicle, bank account, or any asset you may have. If they are done correctly Charging Orders will work for businesses. But, what about your home, vehicles, bank accounts, jewelry and other things of value? Insurance is the answer. It is the best thing you can ever have, there are many different structural types of insurance policies. Knowing what type of coverage, you need is very important. Such as, if you are manufacturing products, you should have liability insurance in the event your product injures a consumer or becomes harmful.

Property Insurance is needed, if your home, the building you are doing business out of, rental property, or any personal property were to be destroyed for any reason, they need to be insured. Insurance is the best asset protection in the world, and absolutely necessary in the business world. Insurance Agents must be part of your mastermind Team.

QUICK BOOKS

Quick Books is a Bookkeeping software, that can be downloaded to any electronic device. This type of accounting is great for new entrepreneurs and investors, there are many different types of accountant software, any one of them will do the job.

New entrepreneurs and investors can keep track of money coming in and money going out, you can pay all your bills through this software, and know exactly how much is in your business account at all times. This software basically communicates with your bank account. This is a great tool for anyone looking to achieve success, this is another financial secret the wealthy utilize. Knowing how much is coming in and going out is a major key to operating a successful business, just go to **www.quickbooks.com** or google search "accounting software" to find alternative software."

You will still need a CPA, but this is what keeps you on top of everything your CPA is doing. So if you believe your CPA is not being very ethical, this is how you can keep track of their every move.

APPLICATION INFORMATION

When requesting credit from vendors, and they require you to fill out an application of any kind, adhere the following advice:

If an application ask for your Social Security Number, never give it up. Give them your "Duns number;" "Experian BIN" or your "Equifax EFX ID" number. Anyone of these numbers will do, you can even use your EIN number that you received from the IRS. The reason for using these numbers and not your personal Social Security number, is because these vendors are dealing with your corporation and not you personally, plus you want to build your business credit, so you need them to report directly to these agencies.

THE BIGGEST MARKETS IN THE WORLD
1) The Derivatives Market
2) The Currency Market
3) The Bond Market
4) The Stock Market
5) The Commodities Market
6) The Real Estate Market

THE DERIVATIVE MARKET is really the insurances market, but most of its weight comes from the Stock Exchange. The derivative market entails more than 700 Trillion.

THE CURRENCY MARKET is currency trading known as the "Foreign Exchange" (FOREX) buying and selling currencies from all over the world. The FOREX has an estimated trading volume of 4 Trillion dollars per day.

THE BOND MARKET is also a trading market, where corporations and governments all over the world are selling bonds to the public. Unlike a shareholder that has a claims to the corporations through stock certificates; bond holders only have IOUs from governments and corporations, there is no ownership, or claim privileges.

THE STOCK MARKET There are multiple Stock Markets all over the world, that are trading, buying and selling stock certificates of companies. Almost every country has at least one stock market. In the United States the majority of the Stock Markets are on Wall Street.

THE COMMODITIES MARKET is worldwide. It sponsors the buying, selling and trading of bulk goods, such as food, oil, gold, natural gas, rubber, iron and more. Countries that produce extensive amounts of these commodities usually sell them to the rest of the world. The Commodities market is very large.

THE REAL ESTATE MARKET is the buying and selling of real property, bare land, undeveloped land, government land, residential land, commercial land, industrial land and other types of properties. Real estate is primary wealth, which makes the real estate market the most important market of all.

CONNECTING WITH OVERSEAS SUPPLIERS

When you are looking to do business with overseas companies, one of the first things you have to do is identify the country that has the product you are looking for. Not every country has every product, one of the best ways to locate the product you are looking for is trade publication.

SUBSCRIBING TO TRADE PUBLICATIONS

If you are interested in finding suppliers from the fare east. Countries like: Burma; Cambodia; China; Hong Kong; Japan; Laos; Macau; Malaysia; Philippines; Singapore; South Korea; Taiwan; Thailand, or; Vietnam. "Global Sources" formerly known as "Asian Sources," is the best publication covering this part of the world. (www.globalsources.com)

Here is a short list of available industry specific publications offered by Global Sources:
*   Auto Parts & Accessories
*   Baby & Children Products;
*   Computer Products;

* Electronic Components;
* Electronics;
* Fashion Apparel & Footwear;
* Gifts & Premiums;
* Home Products;
* LED & Solar Products
* Machinery & Parts;
* Medical & Health Products;
* Security Products;
* Telecom Products.

USING THE INTERNET TO FIND OVERSEAS SUPPLIERS

www.asianproducts.com is another great publication that offers catalogs that provide information on where to buy a wide selection of industry products.

www.etradechannel.net Trade Channel is a great resource for finding suppliers worldwide.

www.kompass.com Kompass is a database of 1.5 million companies representing 23 million products.

www.tradekey.com is a global e-commerce site and has a presence in many countries around the world. Tradekey connects you with global wholesalers, buyers, importers, exporters, manufacturers and distributors in more than 240 countries.

www.mfg.com is a marketplace where buyers purchase industrial goods, and also make a Request for Quotation (RFQ) to have textile & apparel products made to specifications to fit your specific needs. MFG will match your RFQ with suppliers around the world that have the right equipment, and expertise to produce your product.

www.tradeindia.com is an online business-to-business website for small businesses located in India. They provide information about buyers and sellers from India for a wide variety of products.

www.alibaba.com Alibaba is an online marketplace for global and domestic Chinese trade. This site connects you with buyers and suppliers from all around the world.

www.sourcing.tdctrade.com The Hong Kong Trade Development Council (HKTDC) enables you to buy and sell products from Hong Kong, mainland China and Taiwan. This site gives you information on banking and finance, electronics, garments, textiles, gift and housewares, communication technology, timepieces, jewelry, optical products, toys, and sporting goods.

www.wand.com Wand is an advance directory indexing system that can help match buyers and sellers in every industry and country around the world.

FINDING UNITED STATES SUPPLIERS

You can locate suppliers in the United States through trade magazines or newspapers, online references and specific trade directories.

www.thomasnet.com The Thomas Register is a comprehensive directory of American manufacturers and distributors. The Thomas register is a publication, and can be accessed online or by phone at (212)695-0500. This company has information, catalogs, contact information on almost every company in America, foreign companies always look to the Thomas register for United States business information.

www.wand.com Wand is again shown here, because it is one of the internets most advanced product category system for matching buyers and sellers in every industry. Buyers visiting this site can search for a list of qualified suppliers for specific products. Here is a sample list of the type of products the suppliers listed offer:

* Agriculture & Forestry
* Arts, Crafts & Hobbies
* Automotive
* Books, Music & Video
* Building & Construction
* Chemicals & Organic
* Clocks & Watches
* Communications
* Computer & Technology
* Consumer Electronics
* Education & Training
* Electrical & Electronics
* Environmental Equipment
* Fashion & Apparel
* Fine Art, Antiques & Collectibles
* Food & Beverages
* Gift & Jewelry
* Home & Garden
* Industrial Equipment
* Medical
* Metals
* Minerals, Mining & Drilling
* Office Equipment
* Packaging
* Personal Care Products
* Photography
* Plastic & Rubber
* Safety & Security
* Science and Technology
* Service Equipment
* Sports and Recreation
* Textile & Leather
* Toys & Games
* Transportation

www.exusa.thinkglobal.us Export USA provides worldwide exposure for U.S. products. This is a great site with a large variety of industry categories and products that can be bought and sold to the rest of the world.

Exportyellowpages.comcom The Export Yellow Pages is a reference tool that foreign buyers use to locate U.S. goods and services. It is basically an electronic matchmaking program. The Yellow Pages let you present your products to foreign buyers at no cost. This site is an online directory of U.S. exporters and export service providers.

www.akama.com Akama is where you can find businesses, products, reviews and deals from all over the United States. This tool can be used to detail information about companies and

connect those companies to their consumers.
www.otexa.ita.doc.gov/madeinusa Otexa is the office of textiles and apparel. The purpose of this database is to list United States Manufacturers, suppliers, and contractors to assist those seeking to locate/source textiles, apparel, and footwear products made in the United States.

FREIGHT FOWARDERS

If you are planning to buy products from overseas suppliers and ship them back to your country, or if you are planning to ship goods from your country to other countries, a freight forwarder will handle this part of the business for you. Contact them at: **www.forwarders.com**; **www.portal.freightgate.com**; **www.freightnet.com**. Freight forwarders can handle all your shipping needs, such as, dealing with custom agents documentation, making sure your shipment arrive on time; and making sure the product is in good condition.

If there are any products out there that you would like to add to your business catalog but do not know where to find it, simply look at the tag or package labeling to identify which country it was made; then go to "Alibaba.com" and input the information in the search browser, hundreds of companies that make that same product will appear on your screen.

One example is: if you type in "Polo shirts made in China"; you will receive hundreds of results of companies that manufacture polo shirts. Then you have a choice to contact any number of these companies, and ask for a catalog and pricing list. Remember to search until you find the best price with the best quality of textile, most of those companies will negotiate all of their prices.

Alibaba.com and **Aliexpress.com** are both owned by the

Alibaba Group but they have two different business models. **Alibaba.com** is a business to business (B2B) site that provide a trading platform for buyers and sellers to exchange information, so they may trade in large quantities.

www.aliexpress.com on the other hand is for smaller businesses interested in sourcing smaller quantities as few as one item.

You can request product samples before you make any purchase in order to have the product inspected to make sure it is safe for human consumption. (**www.us.sgs.com**) You can send products and have them inspected, SGS is the worlds leading inspecting, verification, testing and certification company. They can also be reached by calling (201)508-3000.

RESOURCE LINKS

* Trademark Links
www.uspto.gov

* Virtual Office
www.alliancevirtualoffice.com
www.re9us.com/virtual-office

* Tax ID
www.irs.gov/business

* Corporate Set-Up Assistance
www.legalzoom.com   www.mcorporation.com
www.incorTorate.com   www.bizfiling.com
www.incforfree.com   www.mycompany.com

* Logo / Website / Slogan / Business Plan
www.fiverr.com   www.freelogoservices.com

* 411 Directories
www.listyourself.net   www.expressupdate.com/search
www.yellowpages.com   www.superpages.com
www.neustarlocaleze.biz   www.infousa.com
www.smallbusiness.yahoo.com/loca1-listin

* Phone Services
www.ringcentral.com   wuw.vonage.com/business
www.att.com/gen/landingpage

*Merchant Services

www.clover.com	www.squareup.com

*Business Plan

www.sbaggov/business-guide/plan/wirte-your-business-21an-template

*Business License Permit

www.businesslicense.com	www.licensesuite.com/search
www.cityapplications.com/index.html

www.sba.9ov/businees-guide/launch/apply-for-license7permits-federal-state

*Third Party Bureaus

www.factualdata.com	www.cortera.com
www.paynet.com	www.accurint.com
www.chexsystems.com	www.hardmoneylender.com

SECRETARY OF STATE LINKS

Alabama	www.sos.alabama.gov
Alaska	www.commerce.alaska.gov
Arizona	www.azsos.gov
Arkansas	www.5os.arkan5a5.gov
California	www.sos.ca.gov
Colorado	www.sos.state.co.us
Connecticut	www.ct.gov
Delaware	www.corp.delaware.gov
District of Columbia	www.os.dc.gov
Florida	www.myflorida.com/sunbiz
Georgia	www.sos.ga.gov
Hawaii	www.cca.hawaii.gov
Idaho	www.sos.idaho.gov
Illinois	www.cyberdriveillinois.com
Indiana	www.in.gov/sos
Iowa	www.sos.iowa.gov
Kansas	www.kssos.org
Kentucky	www.sos.ky.gov
Louisiana	www.sos.la.gov
Maine	www.maine.gov/sos
Maryland	www.sos.maryland.gov
Massachusetts	www.sec.state.ma.us/cor
Michigan	www.michigan.gov
Minnesota	www.sos.state.mn.us
Mississippi	www.sos.ms.gov

Missouri	www.sos.mo.gov
Montana	www.sos.mt.gov
Nebraska	www.sos.ne.gov
Nevada	www.nvsos.gov
New Hampshire	www.sos.nh.gov
New Jersey	www.nj.gov/state
New Mexico	www.sos.state.nm.us
New York	www.dos.ny.gov
North Carolina	www.sosnc.gov
North Dakota	www.sos.nd.gov
Ohio	www.sos.state.oh.us
Oklahoma	www.sos.ok.gov
Oregon	www.sos.oregon.gov
Pennsylvania	dos
Rhode Island	www.sos.ri.gov
South Carolina	www.sos.sc.gov
South Dakota	www.sdsos.gov
Tennessee	www.sos.tn.gov
Texas	www.sos.state.tx.us
Utah	www.utah.gov
Vermont	www.sec.state.vt.us
Virginia	www.commonwealth.virginia.gov
Washington	www.sos.wa.gov
West Virginia	www.sos.wv.gov
Wisconsin	www.sos.state.wi.us
Wyoming	www.soswy.state.wy.us

OTHER SOUCES OF FUNDING

* Using personal credit
* Vendor and revolving account
* Account receivables financing
* SBA Loans
* Revenue credit lines
* Private funds financing
* Real Estate financing
* Revenue lending
* Equipment financing
* Sign and wrap financing
* 401K Loans
* Collateral financing
* Equipment leasing
* Crowd funding
* Merchant advances

            And many many more!!!

ABOUT THE AUTHOR

Jonathan Wainwright has given the whole world a new outlook on themselves and wealth. He has studied world economics and the mental perception of money. He has also spent many years following the economic rise and fall of ordinary people, wealthy people, and politicians.

We Help You Self-Publish Your Book
You're The Publisher and We're Your Legs.
We Offer Editing For An Extra Fee, and Highly
Suggest It, If Waved, We Print What You Submit!

Crystell Publications is not your publisher, but we will help you self-publish your own novel.

Don't have all your money? …. No Problem!
Ask About our Payment Plans
Crystal Perkins, MHR
Essence Magazine Bestseller
We Give You Books!
PO BOX 8044 / Edmond – OK 73083
www.crystalstell.com
(405) 414-3991

Plan 1-A 190 - 250 pgs. $719.00	Plan 1-B 150 -180 pgs. $674.00
Plan 1-C 70 - 145pgs $625.00	
2 (Publisher/Printer) Proofs, Correspondence, 3 books, Manuscript Scan and Conversion, Typeset, Masters, Custom Cover, ISBN, Promo in Mink, 2 issues of Mink Magazine, Consultation, POD uploads. 1 Week of E-blast to a reading population of over 5000 readers, book clubs, and bookstores, The Authors Guide to Understanding The POD, and writing Tips, and a review snippet along with a professional query letter will be sent to our top 4 distributors in an attempt to have your book shelved in their bookstores or distributed to potential book vendors. After the query is sent, if interested in your book, distributors will contact you or your outside rep to discuss shipment of books, and fees.	

Plan 2-A 190 - 250 pgs. $645.00	Plan 2-B 150 -180 pgs. $600.00
Plan 2-C 70 - 145pgs $550.00	
1 Printer Proof, Correspondence, 3 books, Manuscript Scan and Conversion, Typeset, Masters, Custom Cover, ISBN, Promo in Mink, 1 issue of Mink Magazine, Consultation, POD upload.	

www.ingramcontent.com/pod-product-compliance
Lightning Source LLC
Chambersburg PA
CBHW020422220526
45464CB00002B/527